THE LAST DAYS

BIBLE PROPHECIES OF THE
END TIMES REVEALED

BY

RUSSELL COLLINS

Copyright 2011 – Russell Collins

All Rights Reserved. This book is protected under the copyright laws of the United States of America. It may not be copied or reprinted for commercial gain or profit. Short quotations or occasional page copying for personal or group study is permitted and encouraged.

Unless otherwise noted, Scripture quotations are from the King James Version of the Bible.

For Worldwide Distribution

Printed in the United States of America

ISBN – 978-0-615-30248-5

Deep South Publishing
41 Phillips Street
Swainsboro, Georgia

TABLE OF CONTENTS

CHAPTER ONE – END TIME PROPHECIES FULLFILLED 5

CHAPTER TWO – PROPHECIES UNFOLDING NOW 19

CHAPTER THREE – THE RAPTURE 33

CHAPTER FOUR – THE WAR WITH GOG AND MAGOG 45

CHAPTER FIVE – THE ANTICHRIST.. 55

CHAPTER SIX – THE GREAT TRIBULATION........................... 67

CHAPTER SEVEN – MID-TRIBULATION 87

CHAPTER EIGHT – ARMAGEDDON 105

CHAPTER NINE – THE MILLENIUM 115

CHAPTER TEN – THE NEW HEAVEN AND EARTH............... 129

INTRODUCTION

Biblical prophecies that are recorded in the Bible started over six thousand years ago. The early prophecies were made by God when He spoke to his servants and told them of the things that would come to pass. Later He would speak through His prophets and they would prophecy to the people of things that come to pass in a short time or even hundreds of years in the future.

Some of the major prophets were Jeremiah, Isaiah, Ezekiel and Daniel. A lot of other prophets were called minor prophets such as Amos, Ezra, Hosea, Zechariah, Zephaniah, Micah and Nahum.

There are over twenty five hundred prophecies that are listed in the Bible and around two thousand have already been fulfilled. The amazing thing about all the prophecies given, is the fact that all that have been fulfilled so far, have been one hundred percent correct just as they were predicted they would.

In our present day we have those who prophecy about things that will come to pass and are considered to be a kind of modern day prophet. The sad thing about this is that a lot of the things that they predict to come to pass have failed to do so. This is the sign of a false prophet. When a true prophet predicts that certain things will come to pass, it always does. A true prophet of God is never wrong in their predictions. When God uses a person to prophecy, it always comes to pass one hundred percent of the time.

More people today are interested in Bible prophecy than ever before. The main reason is that we are living in an age where people are actually seeing prophecies fulfilled. Books on Bible prophecy sales are at an all time high. The Left Behind series of books and movies has had a big impact about the interest about the end times. A person can read a prophecy book along with the Bible and get excited when they realize that some of the prophecies written twenty five hundred years ago have been fulfilled in their lifetime.

Pastors and TV Evangelists are preaching about the end times in their sermons. When a sermon is preached on the end times, there seems to be an excitement in the air when the good news that Jesus could return for the church at any time. There is a great need today for all evangelical churches to be preaching and teaching about the prophecies of the Bible that are being fulfilled and that Jesus could come at any time. Churches that preach about Jesus coming again on a regular basis has an excitement about them and scores of people are being saved. I believe that if Jesus literally spoke to the Christian people of today that he would tell us to tell everyone that He is coming soon and lead people to be saved. What more important message than this could there be?

I believe that we are living in the most exciting time in all of history. More Bible prophecies about the end times have been fulfilled in the last fifty or sixty years than have been fulfilled in the last nineteen hundred years. Prophecies that were made over twenty five hundred years ago have finally been fulfilled in the last century. For hundreds of years Bible scholars have said that Jesus could return at any time and the rapture of the church would take place. They were sincere in believing this, but certain prophecies had to be fulfilled in order for this to take place.

Prophecies from the books of Isaiah, Ezekiel and Zechariah predicted that someday the Jews would return to their homeland of Israel and possess their land again. This did not happen until Israel was officially declared a nation in May of 1948. This happened just as Isaiah prophesied it would when he declared that Israel would become a nation in one day. Jews have been migrating to Israel steadily for nearly a century. A mass number of Jews from the Soviet countries started arriving there when the Soviet Union fell in 1991. God opened the door then and now He is allowing it to slow down due to Russia beginning to return to the old ways of controlling their people. This is just another sign of the end times coming to pass and Jesus returning for his people.

In the book of Zephaniah, it was prophesied that the Jews would begin to use the Hebrew language again and this came to pass in the 1900s.

Isaiah prophesied that the land of Israel would return to prosperity and that trees again would grow there and also that the nation would fill all the world with fruit. This has come to pass for now Israel is one of the leading producers of fruit in the world.

God gave the people of Israel knowledge of creating irrigation systems in their land that turned the deserts and barren land into a land that grows beautiful trees and many kinds of fruit for their economy.

In the book of Daniel, it tells us that in the last days that knowledge would increase. In the last seventy five years it seems that knowledge has increased to the extent that it amazes everyone at the rate that inventions are coming to pass.

In the little nation of Israel, God has given them access to new technology so that they now have a modern army and defense system that is second to no one. Many nations have tried to defeat Israel in the past few years, but no one has succeeded in overthrowing God's chosen people.

Many people today do not read Bible prophecy books because they feel that prophecy books are so complicated and deep that they will have a hard time understanding scripture references pertaining to end time prophecies that they will not attempt to purchase and read these books.

This book is written using simple words so that even a fifth grader can understand the prophecies about the end times. All scripture references are taken from the King James version of the Bible which is a favorite with most everyone who is interested in reading God's word.

I hope that this book will be a blessing to anyone who reads it and may God bless each of you.

The Last Days

CHAPTER ONE

END TIME PROPHECIES FULLFILLED

More prophecies of the Bible have been fulfilled since the year 1900 than over the last 2000 years. By the year 1900 Jews had started to slowly migrate to the land of Israel from all over the world, although there was not an official state for them to live in during this period. The Jews had been without a homeland to call their own for over 2500 years. By the year 1900 there were about 40,000 that moved into the land which is known now as Israel. Today approximately 6 million living there and more are entering the country each day.

Most all prophecies of the Bible are connected some way with the Nation of Israel.

PROPHECIES FULLFILLED SINCE THE YEAR 1900

The prophet Isaiah said that God would restore Israel and make it a place where flowers would bloom and plantations would flourish. Through irrigation and working on the land the Jews have turned barren land into some of the richest land known in the entire world. Israel is now one of the leading food producers in the world. Some of the food products that they produce are wheat, peas, sunflowers, grapes, wine, peanuts, grapefruit, oranges, lemons and peaches. They also produce quality cotton that is shipped all over the world.

God has given the Jewish People the knowledge and wisdom to turn a barren land into one of the leading exporters in the world. The nation of Israel is small in size but, it produces more products per square mile than almost any nation in the world today.

ISAIAH 51:3 - For the Lord will comfort Zion: he will comfort all her waste places; and he will make her wilderness like Eden, and her desert like the garden of the Lord; joy and gladness will be found therein, thanksgiving, and the voice of melody.

ISAIAH 27:6 - He shall cause them that come of Jacob to take root: Israel shall blossom and bud, and fill the face of the world with fruit.

ISAIAH 41:18-20 - I will open rivers in high places, and fountains in the midst of the valleys: I will make the wilderness a pool of water and the dry land springs of water. I will plant in the wilderness the cedar, the shittah tree, and the myrtle, and the oil tree; I will set in the desert the fir tree, and the pine and the box tree together. That they may see, and know, and consider, and understand together, that the hand of the Lord hath done this, and the Holy One of Israel hath created it.

KNOWLEDGE WOULD INCREASE

From the time of Jesus to the beginning of the 20th Century that inventions and better ways of doing things were hardly moving. Things seemed to start moving at the turn of the century when inventions were coming on the scene. Electricity, telephones, automobiles, appliances, airplanes, better medicines and farm equipment brought into being a much higher standard of living that had never been thought of as being possible.

After World War Two, things seemed to speed up and all kinds of new inventions were on the market. Today, knowledge is increasing so fast that it is mind boggling. Things like man going to the moon, computers, the internet, trains going 200 miles per hour, cell phones, GPS systems, medical breakthroughs and food being produced in record quantities.

As the population of the earth increased, God knew that man was going to need some help to handle the problems that would come in to being. For instance, the transactions of sales in a store that normally would be done by using a pencil to record sales of products. He gave man the knowledge to invent the computer that could be used to record transactions by using bar codes on products sold. The satellites that are orbiting the earth allow TV programs and the internet to function with speed and accuracy. These are just a few of the examples of the prophecy of Daniel about the increase of knowledge in the last days.

DANIEL - 12:4 - But thou, O Daniel, shut up the words, and seal the book, even to the time of the end: many shall run to and fro, and knowledge shall be increased.

ISRAEL BECOMES A NATION IN ONE DAY

In May 14, 1948 the state of Israel come into existence. This meant that the land of Palestine would no longer be one country but two states, one Jewish and one Arab. The Jews accepted the UN resolution while the Arabs rejected it. The European Jews began arriving with no money and little belongings, but they were in the new land that God had promised them many years before.

The very next day the Arabs started attacking the Jews. The Jews had very little military operations and were outnumbered, but they still defended their new nation. Over the next few years, Egypt, Syria, Jordan, Lebanon and Iraq continued to attack Israel, but Israel still held on to their country. The Arabs would not admit to the fact that in the scriptures it was written by the prophets that the Jews would have a nation and they would not be defeated. This is true today. The Palestinians want all of the land that the Jews live on.

ISAIAH 66:8 - Who have heard such a thing? Who have seen such things? Shall the earth be made to bring forth in one day? Or shall a nation be born at once? For as soon as Zion travailed, she brought forth her children.

THE SIX DAY WAR OF 1967

The six day war of 1967 started on June 5th. 1967. By 1967 the Israeli army had become a much improved army and was ready to defend their country. The countries attacking Israel were Egypt, Jordan and Syria with the countries of Iraq, Kuwait, Saudi Arabia, Sudan and Algeria giving aid to the Arabs.

The first strikes of the six - day - war happened when the Israeli Air Force attacked Egypt after hearing of the planned attack by Egypt. The Israeli planes destroyed over 400 Egyptian planes before they could take off from their airfield. After this attack, the Israeli troops and planes began attacking the other hostile countries before they could get their armies together and destroyed them all. The war only lasted a total of 6 days.

The Arabs and their coalition had a total of 570,000 troops, 3000 tanks and 985 jets. The total population of Israel at that time was 2,000,000.

The Israeli soldiers told of things that happened during the war that would have to be considered miracles and could only have happened through the works of God.

Before the 6 day war, the city of Jerusalem was controlled by the Arabs. The Dome of the Rock used for Muslim worship is located on the Temple mount where the original Jewish temple was. According to scripture there will be another Jewish temple built on this location. In Matthew 24:15, Jesus tells of the Antichrist standing in the holy place (which means a temple) and declaring that he is God. No one knows exactly when the temple will be built, but the Jewish victory in the 6 day war made it possible to obtain the land in Jerusalem for the temple to be rebuilt. More details of the rebuilding of the temple will be found in another chapter.

PSALM 83:3-8 - They have taken crafty counsel against thy people, and consulted against thy hidden ones. They have said, come, and let us cut them off from being a nation; that the name of Israel may be no more in remembrance. For they have consulted together with one consent: they are confederate against thee. The tabernacles of Edom and the Ishmaelites of Moaband the Hagarenes; Gebal, and Ammon, and Amalek; the Philistines with the inhabitants of Tyre; Assur also is joined with them: they have helped the children of Lot, Selah.

The nations named in the Old Testament in Psalm 83 above have modern names of Egypt, Saudi Arabia, Iraq, Syria, Lebanon and Jordan.

REBIRTH OF THE HEBREW LANGUAGE

Eliezer Ben-Yehuda was one of the first Zionists and is credited with the revival of Hebrew as a modern tongue spoken by a renascent Jewish nation. He was born in Lithuania in 1858. At the age of seventeen he had a revelation about what a common language is to a nation. He then took on the task of reviving the Hebrew language for it had slowly been forgotten through the centuries. He took a teaching position in Jerusalem and began teaching courses in Hebrew. He became the forerunner of the Hebrew Language Academy. In 1910 he published the first of six volumes of 'The Complete Dictionary of Ancient and Modern Hebrew'. This was the beginning of the reviving of the original Hebrew and has become the official language of Israel again.

ZEPHANIAH 3:9 - For then will I turn to the people a pure language, that they may all call upon the name of the Lord, to serve him with one consent.

In the book of Matthew, chapter 24, Jesus Himself gave many prophecies pertaining to the end times. All prophecies through verse 14 have been fulfilled already. Any person living today should realize that we are living in the end times when they read these verses of scripture. It seems like reading a newspaper article when you compare it to the prophecies that Jesus gives us in this chapter.

FALSE CHRISTS

MATTHEW 24:5 - For many will come in My name, saying "I am the Christ, and will deceive many."

MATTHEW 24:11 - And many false prophets shall rise, and shall deceive many. In the last 2 centuries there have been more claims by people saying that they are Christ than any other period of time. Cults are on the increase all over the world. A cult is any religion that has been started by someone other than Jesus. Satan has used many individuals as puppets to start a movement of some kind and claim that they are really Jesus in the flesh.

One such movement was started by a man named Jim Jones. He was born in 1931 in Crete, Indiana and was the founder of The People's Temple Full Gospel Church an off shoot of the Christian Church (Disciples of Christ). After forming a group of over 1000 members he became under investigation for allegation rights abuses. He then convinced the group to move Guyana, South America in 1977 where he used their money to set up a settlement and convinced the people that he was their God. He used mind control and members would do anything he asked.

In 1977, Congressman Leo Ryan went to Jonestown in Guyana to investigate allegations of rights abuse. Ryan and several others were killed at the airport when they were ready to return to the U.S. After this Jones convinced his congregation that then was the time they should follow him as an example and partake of poison. The death toll was 913 men, women and children. Jones took his life that day with a gunshot wound to the head.

All over the world today, men are claiming to be Jesus and what is so sad is the fact that people are believing that they are really Jesus in the flesh. Jesus said that they would come on the scene and say" I am the Christ."

Another movement is called "The New Age Movement". They claim that there are a lot of ways to get to heaven other than Jesus Christ. Jesus said in his word "I am the way the truth and the life, no man comes to the father except by me." Many are deceived into thinking that they are really a type of God themselves and that they answer to no one except themselves.

It seems that every day some religious cult comes on the scene and is leading people down the path of destruction. People have to remember that religion did not die on the cross for you - Jesus did.

MATTHEW 24:6-7 "And you will hear of wars and rumors of wars. See that you are not troubled; for all these things must come to pass, but the end is not yet. For nation will rise against nation, and kingdom against kingdom. And there will be famines, pestilences, and earthquakes in various places."

Since Jesus spoke these verses over 2 thousand years ago, there have been many wars, but none have been as devastating as those that have taken place in the last two hundred years. The Civil War in the United States was bad, but they seemed to be getting worse and bigger. When World War I and World War II came along, more powerful weapons of war was used. Planes with bombs, tanks, all types of guns and at the close of World War II the atomic bomb was used to bring the war to a close. Then came the Korean conflict, the Vietnamese conflict and the Iraq war. All over the globe wars are popping up and rumors of wars are being talked about every day. No time in recorded history has the number of countries seem to be ready to go to war with one another. We are living in the end times and Matthew Chapter 24 confirms that this prophecy is being fulfilled daily.

FAMINES, PESTILENCES AND EARTHQUAKES

At no time in history has mankind been able to see things around the world as they literally happen. Television seemed to be a miracle at the time it was invented, but when God allowed man to put satellites in orbit to work with television, the world became so small. We can now see with our own eyes the many horrible things that are happening to people around the world. We see people dying every day in countries where food is so scarce that very little is available to survive on. It is estimated that 18,000 people are dying every day because of starvation. Nations around the world are sending food to starving countries, but so much of it fall by the wayside due to warlords confiscating it and hoarding it themselves. Jesus said that this would happen in the last days and in our lifetime it is coming true.

Pestilences and disease are going rampart in so many nations around the world. The word HIV is so frightening nowadays and rightly so because of the deadly disease that it is. Millions are dying year after year from Aids, especially in the Africa where some countries have a population that is over 50 percent HIV. It seems that a new disease is discovered every day around the world. They are occurring faster than man can come up with a cure.

Cancer was hardly heard of until after World War II. It seemed to spring up and spread like wildfire. The cure has been slow to this horrible disease. People often wonder how it seems to occur in the body of so many people. Eating habits, food additives and air pollution have been said to be partly to blame. No one really knows, but the one thing that is for sure is that Jesus prophesied that this would happen in it is.

There has never been as many earthquakes recorded as there have been in the last 50 years. The largest earth-quake recorded on the Richter scale was 9.5 that happened in Chile in 1960. Earthquakes have been devastating in all parts of the world and the bad thing about some of them is that when they happen in the ocean they cause a Tsunami which is a huge tidal wave that travels sometimes at 500 miles per hour. The highest tidal wave happened at the Fairweather Fault in Alaska in 1958. The height was estimated at 1720 feet tall.

On Dec. 26, 2004 an earthquake off the coast of Sumatra, Indonesia caused the most destruction in modern day history. It has been estimated that the force of this earthquake was comparable to 23,000 atomic bombs going off at one time. It caused a tsunami that developed a tidal wave that traveled at 500 miles and hour at times and killed 227,898 people. An earthquake happened on Feb. 27, 2010 in Chile leaving more than 800 people dead.

In the year 2011, a huge earthquake happened in Japan causing thousands of deaths. It was one of the highest recorded on the Richter scale. This earthquake shook the foundations of several nuclear plants causing radiation leaks and came close to a major disaster.

Tornadoes ripped through the Southeastern parts of the United States killing over three hundred people. The Mississippi River over flowed and all the states that it ran through suffered loss of thousands of homes, crops of grain costing millions of dollars.

There seems to be more and more earthquakes, hurricanes and tornadoes happening ever year, confirming prophecies in the Bible are coming true. It just proves that if something is written in God's word it will always come true.

THE GOSPEL OF THE KINGDOM
PREACHED IN ALL THE WORLD

The Gospel of Jesus Christ has now been preached in all the countries of the world. At the turn of the century this was something that seemed impossible, but with modern day communications, technology and various inventions have made it possible. When the disciples of Jesus and Paul were teaching about the gospel, everything was done by word of mouth or by writing letters. Travel in those days was by ship, horses, camels and walking. It is so different now with the use of travel by planes, railroads, autos and huge ships. One of the greatest tools to spread the gospel nowadays is by satellite TV. By the use of the satellites in orbit around the world today, live TV programs can be delivered to any country on earth. A lot of the TV evangelists on the airways now say that every country in the world is now being reached daily.

The Gideon International now has camps in over 190 countries where Bibles and Testaments are being handed out daily at the rate of about 1 every second. They are now able to produce Bibles in 93 different languages. There are more missionaries on the field now than ever before spreading the gospel. Thousands every day now are being saved by hearing the gospel.

Some would say that every person has not heard the message. This is true and billions of people have never heard the gospel, but the scripture says that the gospel would preached in all the world, not to every person. This is another prophecy that has came true in our lifetime.

Matt. 24:14 - And this gospel of the kingdom shall be preached in all the world for a witness unto all nations; and then shall the end come.

SIGNS OF THE END TIMES

Matthew 24:32-33 tells the parable of the fig tree, about when its branch has already become tender and puts forth leaves, you know that summer is near. In 1948 when Israel became a nation again this was the most important sign yet. This parable tells us that Israel is the fig tree and that the Jews returning are the leaves that is spoken of. Jesus says that when the leaves appear then you know that summer is near. The year 1948 is the very key that indicates that the end is near. At no time in history has there been the awareness of how close the coming of the Lord than it is now. Years ago people would say " Christ cannot come now because a lot of the prophecies have not been fulfilled, but this is not the case now. Jesus can come at any minute because all the end time prophecies have been fulfilled or are being fulfilled at the present time."

When Jesus told his disciples this parable of the fig tree, he was telling them that the generation that lived during this time would not pass away because all these things are fulfilled. There are several interpretations of how long a generation is. Some say forty years make up a generation, others say seventy five or even one hundred years. Since 1948, fifty-two years have passed by. So even if one hundred years is the correct length of a generation, this means that Jesus could come any time within the next forty eight years. No one knows the exact date when Jesus returns to take us home, but we do know that it is very near.

MATTHEW 24:32-35 Now learn a parable of the fig tree, When his branch is yet tender, and putteth forth leaves, ye know that summer is nigh: So likewise ye, when ye shall see all these things, know that it is near, even at the doors. Verily I say unto you, This generation shall not pass, till all these things be fulfilled.

DAYS OF NOAH

In the days of Noah, the world was filled with evil people who had no regard of God or his fellow man. It had become so corrupt that God told Noah to build an ark because a flood was on it's way to destroy mankind. The world that we live in today is very similar to the days of Noah. Violence, immorality and other sin seems to dominate every country on the face of the earth.

Jesus told his disciples that the day was coming when man would be doing the same evil things that happened in Noah's time. He has warned people that the same thing would be happening very soon. He destroyed the world with water the first time, but this time it would be by a different method through the wrath of God and the battle of Armageddon.

THE COMING OF APOSTASY

In 2 Timothy, chapter 3, Paul tells of perilous times that will take place in the last days. He tells about the behavior of man and things that man will do during a period of time that leads into the end times. This is not something that is yet to come, it is a prophecy that has come true and is still being fulfilled this very day.

2 TIMOTHY 3:1-7 This know also, that in the last days perilous times shall come. For men shall be lovers of their own selves, covetous, boasters, proud, blasphemers, disobedient to parents, unthankful, unholy, without natural affection trucebreakers, false accusers, incontinent, fierce, despisers of those that are good, traitors, heady, high minded, lovers of pleasures more than lovers of God, having a form of godliness, but denying the power thereof: from such turn away. For of this sort are they which creep into houses, and lead captive silly women laden with sins, led away with divers lusts, ever learning, and never able to come to the knowledge of the truth.

He said that "man would become lovers of themselves." The

old nature that we all have since birth seems to want everything for self. There is an urging through our being to get all that we can of earthly things and just as fast as we can. We seem to put ourselves at the top of the list to satisfy. The word I is the most important thing in lives today.

So many times when men get paid at the end of the week, their first thought is " I have got to get my beer and drugs before I carry any money home to the family." I am going to party until I get my fill." I am going to get this car for my pleasure now and worry about paying for it later."

Paul said that "man would be lovers of money". The phrase that "Money is the root of all evil" is often quoted as coming from the Bible, but it is not. The Bible says that "The love of money is the root of all evil" (1 Timothy 6:10) Money in it's self is not bad. Money is needed for man to use to buy things that are needed for survival. Man in this day and time will do almost anything to obtain wealth. They will cheat, steal, rob and kill for the love of money. The old nature will convince one that they deserve all the money they can get so I will get it no matter what the circumstances are.

Paul said that in the last days man would be covetous, boasters, and proud. Man will covet another man's wife, his home, his boat, his car, his job and any other thing that he does not have and he will do just about anything to get them. Years ago a person who did not have the possessions that his neighbor had would start to save his money and eventually get something like his neighbor. Nowadays is a different story, because he wants it now. When he gets a job he wants to be boss next month. He wants to boast about what he possesses. He is proud and wants other people to see what he has done. These very things were the reason Lucifer was cast out of heaven and became Satan.

Paul said that there would be blasphemers, and disobedient to parents. Using the Lord's name in vain is just a normal thing with most people nowadays. Even 40 years ago most people who cursed were careful not to use the foil language just anywhere. Using the name of God in vain seems to boost some people's ego. They seem to be proud about it and will do this with no respect for anyone.

Many years ago when the movie "Gone with the Wind" came out, the word damn was used and people thought was just too much. How times have changed since then. Just as Paul wrote in his letter to Timothy, blasphemers in the latter days would be heard with no limits as to what is said.

What was unheard of many years ago is now a common thing when so many children and young people are so disobedient toward their parents. They are unthankful and rude and sometimes even murder their own parents.

Paul said that there would be some people who in the end time would be without natural affection toward one another and be drawn into homosexuality. In the latter part of the 1900's, men and women started coming out of the closet and admitting and even bragging about unnatural life style. Gay parades are going on across the country like never before just as it was in the days of Sodom and Gomorrah when God destroyed the cities, He hates this sin now just as much as He did then.

Paul continues to give information about things that will be happening in the end times like trucebreakers, false accusers, incontinent, fierce, despisers of those that are good. There will be traitors, heady, high-minded lovers of pleasures more than lovers of god. All these things have come to pass and are continually happening all over the world today.

2 TIMOTHY 3:1-6 This know also, that in the last days perilous times shall come. For men shall be lovers of their own selves, covetous, boasters, proud, blasphemers, disobedient to parents, unthankful, unholy, without natural affection, trucebreakers, false accusers, incontinent, fierce, despisers of those that are good. Traitors, heady, high-minded lovers of pleasures more than lovers of God. Having a form of godliness, but denying the power thereof: from such turn away.

2 TIMOTHY 4:3-4 For the time will come when they will not endure sound doctrine; but after their own lusts shall they heap to

themselves teachers, having itching ears; and they shall turn away their ears from the truth, and shall be turned unto fables.

CHAPTER TWO

PROPHECIES UNFOLDING NOW

At this present time we are seeing several prophecies unfolding before our very eyes. These are prophecies that have not yet been fulfilled or completed, but are slowly beginning to take place in our lifetime. Some of these are the following:

1 - The rebuilding of the Temple in Jerusalem
2 - The revived Roman Empire
3 - The New World Order

THE REBUILDING OF THE TEMPLE IN JERSAULEM

In the Bible we are told that the First Temple in Jerusalem was built in 957 BC by King Solomon. It was destroyed by the Babylonians in 586 BC.

Construction of the Second Temple began in 538 BC and was finished in 515 BC. This temple was partially destroyed by the actions of Antiochus Epiphanes in 167 BC who desecrated it by slaughtering a dead pig on the alter in defiance to the God of the Jews. It was then renovated by Herod the Great and become known as Herod's Temple. During the Roman occupation of Judah, the Temple remained under control of the Jewish High Priest. It was later destroyed by the Romans in 70 AD during the Siege of Jerusalem. The prophecy that this would happen is found in Matthew 24:1-2 And Jesus went out, and departed from the temple: and his disciples came to him for to show him the buildings of the temple. And Jesus said unto them, See ye not all these things? Verily I say unto you, There shall not be left here one stone upon another, that shall not be thrown down.

The place where the temple was destroyed was vacant until the 7th Century AD when the Dome of the Rock was built for worship by the Islamic people. Today the Muslims have control of this section of land and do not want any Jews to build any type temple on the property.

According to scripture there must be a temple re-built in Jerusalem before Jesus comes to set up His Kingdom after the battle of Armageddon.

MATTHEW 24:15 When ye therefore shall see the abomination of desolation, spoken of by Daniel the prophet, stand in the holy place.

2 THESSALONIANS 2:3-4 Let no man deceive you by any means: for that day shall not come, except there come a falling away first, and that man of sin be revealed, the son of perdition; Who opposeth and exalteth himself above all that is called God, or that is worshipped; so that he as God sitteth in the temple of God, showing himself that he is God.

For over two thousand years the Jewish people have longed for the time when they would have a temple to worship in and give sacrifices to their God. They were scattered all over the world and there seemed no hope of this ever occurring. They did not have a country of their own to live in and land of their own to build a temple. Then in 1948 Israel became a nation. At this time they did not possess the area where the Temple Mount is located now.

In 1967, when all the Muslim Countries around Israel were planning to crush their tiny country, God delivered them by giving them the knowledge they needed to defeat these enemies in just six days which was known as the Six Day War. After defeating their enemies, they now had possession of all Jerusalem including the land where the original temple set over two thousand years ago.

Most historians believe the Dome of the Rock sets on the original site where the Jewish temple used to be. Others believe that the temple was north of this site.

After the war of 1967, the Palestinians have tried to get this land back, but have not been successful. This will never happen according to scripture, because there has to be a temple built on this site.

Most Orthodox Jews do not want the temple rebuilt because of Jesus coming again, but just to have a temple to worship and give sacrifices as they did two thousand years ago.

A movement today has been started by a group of Jews known as The Temple Institute which is an organization in Israel that is focused on re-establishing the Third Temple. It's goal is to rebuild the Third temple on the site that is currently occupied by the Dome of the Rock and to reinstate sacrificial worship.

At the present time there is no way that the Nation of Islam will ever allow the Dome of the Rock to be used or shared with anyone except for worship by the Muslim faith. This building has been in existence for over 1400 years and time is beginning to take it's toil. The very foundation of one of the walls is said to have huge cracks in it that is getting longer and wider each year. Repair on the walls has not been started to this date. The reason for not repairing it could be that no one wants to tamper with it because of its religious history and not wanting to upset any of the original structure.

The Temple Institute is ready to start building the third temple at any time. Over the last few years they have built all the necessary furniture and ritual objects to completely furnish the new temple just as it was two thousand years ago. If the new temple was built today it would only take a matter of days to have everything in place to begin worship. The following items are ready to be used in the new temple:

1. The Golden Candlestick or Menorah. This is a seven foot, seven-branched candelabrum made of pure bronze and covered

with ninety-five pounds of pure gold at a cost of two million dollars. This item holds seven candles that symbolize God's perfection.

2. The Alter of Incense. This item is made of wood and is used for burning incense The high priest would burn sweet incense every morning and evening as he would go in to light the candles on the candelabrum.

3. The Laver of Cleansing. This was a brass vessel that held water used to clean the hands and feet of the priests as they officiated during Temple Sacrifices.

4. The Table of Shewbread. This was a table overlaid with pure gold that held the offering of shewbread and was placed each week by the Levites on this table as a sacrifice to the Lord.

5. The Mizrak. This vessel was made of eight pounds of solid silver and used to catch the blood of sacrificed animals and applied to the horns of the alter.

6. The Alter of Burnt Offering. This was a wooden alter about seven and one half feet square and about three and one half feet high. This alter stood in the courtyard in front of the sanctuary where the high priest would offer an animal without blemish to be sacrificed for the sins of the people.

7. The Silver Trumpets. These trumpets are thirty-six inches and made of silver, inlaid with gold. They were two of them and used for the "calling of the assembly."

There are several other items used also in the temple worship. They include the oil pitcher used to replenish the Menorah, the incense shovel, the incense chalice, the three-pronged fork to arrange offerings on the altar, the measuring cup to measure meal offerings, the silver shovel to remove ashes from the alter and several others to complete the items used in the temple. The items that the high priest will wear have been made and are read to be used.

The Golden Crown for the high priest is made of solid gold

and is ready to be used.

The Breastplate of the high priest is made of gold and has twelve different stones that are inlaid in the breastplate and has the names of the twelve tribes of Israel on them.

Linen robes for the priests that serve in the temple have been made to supply the numerous priests to wear while conducting worship in the Third Temple.

THE RED HEIFER. When The First Temple was built, instructions were given to the Jews to cleanse the temple before using it. The method of cleansing it was to find a red heifer without spot or blemish and without any color hair except red. The heifer was to be killed and burned and the ashes collected and mixed with water, scarlet thread, cedar and hyssop. The priest will take the hyssop and sprinkle the water on the stones of the Temple Mount, the priests, and the Temple vessels to complete the cleansing.

The Jews that are planning the building of the temple have been trying to locate a pure red heifer for years. It has been reported that a heifer had been born in Israel in 1997. Since then others have been reported being found even in the United States. A solid red heifer is a rarity. When inspecting the red heifer, if a single hair that is not red is found it is rejected.

So now it would appear that everything is ready for The Third Temple to be rebuilt. Only one thing is missing and that is The Ark of the Covenant.

THE NEW SANHEDRIN

The Sanhedrin was a group of 70 elders during the time of Moses who were appointed by God through Moses to act as the final authority of any matter that came up during the time of travel after the Jews came out of the land of Egypt. Instead of Moses having to deal with every disagreement of the Jews, God had him to appoint this court. This acts of the Sanhedrin was very similar to that of Supreme Court in the United States of America.

The Sanhedrin started when there was only a tabernacle and

alter erected from time to time as the Jews journeyed to the promised land of Israel. After the first temple was built by Solomon, they would meet in the outer court of the temple to conduct business. By the time of Jesus Christ, the Sanhedrin had great authority in the lives of the Jewish people. They were then made up of Pharisees and Sadducees and the high priest who claimed to know the Jewish law like no one else.

When the temple was finally destroyed in 70 A.D., they continued to meet until 358 A.D. when it was completely dissolved after the Jews were scattered all over the world.

The Temple Institute of Jerusalem is steadily making plans for the rebuilding of the new temple and have even selected a new Sanhedrin to start operating when it is completed. All of the wearing apparel that they will wear has already been made and are ready to go.

THE ARK OF THE COVENANT

While the Jews were camped at Sinai, God commanded Moses to build an ark to carry the stones on which the Ten Commandments were written on. It was approximately four feet long, two feet wide and two feet high. It was made of acacia wood and plated with pure gold, inside and out. The ark had a pure gold covering with two sculpted Cherubs, also made of pure gold. The ark had four gold rings attached, through which two poles also made of acacia wood and coated in gold was used to carry the ark.

Tradition has it that the ark contained the tablets of stone on which the ten commandments were written, Aaron's rod that budded and some manna that was provided by God for the Children of Israel to eat during their journey to the promised land.

The ark was carried by the Jews from one tabernacle to another as they were built on their journeys through the different lands. It was carried with them when they had battles with many countries and towns.

The ark finally found a resting place when Solomon built the first temple. The ark was placed in it and remained there until the temple was destroyed by Babylonians around 585 B.C. The ark disappeared at that time and no record of it ever being found. Several possibilities of the location of the ark are:

1. The Ethiopians claim to have the ark in one of their cities where it was brought by Menelik the son of the Queen of Sheba, whom tradition has it that Solomon and the Queen of Sheba married and he was their offspring. In the city of Axum in Ethiopia, they claim to have the Ark of the Covenant in a church and has been guarded day and night for hundreds of years.

2. Several people in Jerusalem claim that the ark is under the Temple Mount where it was hidden during the invasion of the Babylonians in 585 B.C and it will be brought out when the new temple is built.

3. Some believe that the Ark of the Covenant is in heaven according to Revelation 11:19 And the temple of God was opened in heaven, and there was seen in his temple the ark of his testament: and there were lightings, and voices, and thundering, and an earthquake, and great hail.

The Ark of the Covenant is the only thing lacking to make everything complete as it was in the days of King Solomon. Regardless if the ark is there or not at the time of the rebuilding of the third temple it will be built according to the planners of the new temple.

WHEN WILL THE NEW TEMPLE BE BUILT?

There are many speculations as to when the new temple will be built. Some say that it can be built any time. The one thing that stands in the way right now is the Dome of the Rock. Something would have to happen to it in order for the temple to be built in the same spot. Israel could demand that the Dome of the Rock be torn down, but this would mean war between the Jews and the Arabs.

Some believe that it will be built when the Antichrist agrees to a peace treaty at the beginning of the tribulation and that it could be built within three years before he would stand in the temple and declare that he is God.

Some believe that it will be built after the rapture of the church and the war that Israel has with Gog and Magog as prophesied in the book of Ezekiel has taken place.

Regardless of the time the Third Temple will be built, we know according to scripture that it will be in Jerusalem in time for the Antichrist to stand in it and proclaim that he is God.

THE REVISED ROMAN EMPIRE

In world history it is recorded that there have been six empires that have ruled the known world. They are as follows:

1. EGYPT
2. ASSYRIA
3. BABYLON
4. MEDO- PERSIANS
5. GREECE
5. ROME

In the book of Daniel are details of the empires that were already past, the one that was present and the ones that were to come in the future. The empires of the Assyrians and Egypt had already taken place when Daniel wrote his book. He was actually living in the time of the Babylonian Empire when he prophesied that another nation would defeat them, which would be the Medo - Persian forces.

While Daniel was in captivity in Babylon, King Nebuchadnezzar had a dream and no one could give the interpretation except Daniel.

DANIEL 2:31-43 Thou, O king, sawest, and behold a great image. This great image, whose brightness was excellent, stood before thee; and the form thereof was terrible. This images's head was of fine gold, his breast and his arms of silver, his belly and his thighs of brass, his legs of iron, his feet part of iron and part of clay. Thou sawest till that a stone was cut out without hands, which smote the image upon his feet that were of iron and clay, and brake them to pieces. Then was the iron, the clay, the brass, the silver, and the gold, broken to pieces together, and became like the chaff of the summer threshing floors; and the wind carried them away, that no place was found for them: and the stone that smote the image became a great mountain, and filled the whole earth. This is the dream; and we will tell the interpretation thereof before the king. Thou, O King, art a king of kings; for the God of heaven hath given thee a kingdom, power, and strength, and glory. And wheresoever the children of men dwell, the beasts of the field and the fowls of the heaven hath he given into thine hand, and hath made thee ruler over them all. Thou art this head of gold. And after thee shall arise another kingdom inferior to thee, and another third kingdom of brass, which shall bear rule over all the earth. And the fourth kingdom shall be strong as iron: forasmouth as iron breaketh in pieces and subdueth all things: and as iron that breaketh all these, shall it break in pieces and bruise. And whereas thou sawest the feet and toes, part of potter's clay, and part of iron, the kingdom shall be divided; but there shall be in it of the strength of the iron, forasmuch as thou sawest the iron mixed with miry clay. And as the toes of the feet were part of iron, and part of clay, so the kingdom shall be partly strong, and partly broken. And whereas thou sawest iron mixed with miry clay, they shall mingle themselves with the see of men: but they shall not cleave one to another, even as iron is not mixed with clay. And in the days of these kings shall the God of heaven set up a kingdom, which shall never be destroyed: and the kingdom shall not be left to other people, but it shall break in pieces and consume all these kingdoms and it shall stand for ever. Forasmuch as thou sawest that the stone was cut out of the mountain without hands, and that it brake in pieces the iron, the brass the clay, the silver and the gold: the great God hath made known to the king what shall come to pass thereafter: and the dream is certain, and the interpretation thereof sure.

    Daniel explained to the king of the empires that was to come. The gold head of the statue would be Babylonia. The chest and arms would be the Medo-Persian empire. The belly and thighs would be the Greek empire. The legs and feet would be Rome that would later fall and be revived again in the last days.

The empires are mentioned later in Daniel and are compared to animals.

DANIEL 7:1-9 In the first year of Belshazzar king of Babylon Daniel had a dream and visions of his head upon his bed: then he wrote the dream, and told the sum of the matters. Daniel spake and said, I saw in my vision by night and said, I saw in my vision by night, and, behold, the four winds of the heaven strove upon the great sea. And four great beasts came up from the sea, diverse one from another. The first was like a lion, and had eagle's wings: I beheld till the wings thereof were plucked, and it was lifted up from the earth, and made stand upon the feet as a man, and a man's heart was given to it. And behold another beast, a second, like to a bear, and it raised up itself on one side, and it had three ribs in the mouth of it between the teeth of it: and they said thus unto it, Arise, devour much flesh. After this I beheld, and lo another, like a leopard, which had upon the back of it four wings of a fowl; the beast had also four heads; and dominion was given to it. After this I saw in the night visions, and behold a fourth beast, dreadful and terrible, and strong exceedingly; and it had great iron teeth; it devoured and brake in pieces, and stamped the residue with the feet of it; and it was diverse from all he beasts that were before it; and it had ten horns. I considered the horns, and, behold, there came up among them another little horn, before whom there were three of the first horns plucked up by the roots: and, behold, in this horn were eyes like the eyes of man, and a mouth speaking great things.

Each animal represented an empire as listed below.

1- The first beast like a lion represents Babylon.
2- The second beast like a like a bear represents the Medo-Persians.
3- The third beast like a leopard represents Greece.
4- The fourth beast with huge iron teeth represents the revived Roman Empire in the last days.

The revived Roman Empire would be a beast that would devour the whole earth.

DANIEL- 7:23-24 Thus he said, The fourth beast shall be the fourth kingdom upon earth, which shall be diverse from all kingdoms, and shall devour the whole earth, and shall tread it down, and break it in pieces. And the ten horns out of this kingdom are ten kings that shall arise: and another shall rise after them; and he shall be diverse from the first, and he shall subdue three kings.

In the book of Revelation the apostle John mentions about ten horns which are ten kings that will be controlled by the antichrist.

REVELATION 14:12 And the ten horns which thou sawest are ten kings, which have received no kingdom as yet: but receive power as kings one hour with the beast.

Some believe that the European Union in Europe will be the kings that is spoken of in Revelation. These countries were established in 1951. The first countries were Belgium, France, Germany, Greece, Italy, the Netherlands, Luxembourg, Ireland, Denmark, United Kingdom, Portugal and Spain. This group of countries could really be called The United States of Europe. Since the beginning of the E.U., they have added other countries for a total of 27. These countries have their own currency which is called the Euro. They have their own constitution which does not contain any reference to Christianity.

Some believe that the ten kings spoken of in the Bible is ten super nations. This would be made up of ten groups of nations around the world. Some have thought of them as being the following:

North America	Latin America
Western Europe	North Africa and Middle East
Japan	Tropical Africa
Australia and South Africa	Southeast Asia
Russia and Eastern Europe	China

According to prophecy, the ten nations to be ruled by the Antichrist seem to be slowly being fulfilled at the present time. One of the main things the E.U. has been looking for and has not yet found is a leader who all nations would be in favor of. Soon a man with all the qualities they are looking for will come on the scene and will be named as the world leader. He will be none other than the Antichrist.

THE NEW WORLD ORDER

The new world order is a term used to describe the uniting of the worlds super powers to secure and maintain global peace. It has been in the making for hundreds and hundreds of years. Leaders of nations around the world would dream about a time when all the world would be under the rule of one man. This would mean no more wars because all countries would be under control of one dictator.

These ideas continued to be thought of all down through the years and in the 1900s, the present name of the new world order came into existence. In 1933, on the back of a one dollar it was written in Latin under the picture of the pyramid "NOVUS ORDO NECLORUM "meaning a new world order. It is still on our one dollar bills today.

The new world order is promoted by the United Nations, The Bilderberg Group, The Council on Foreign Relations and many more around the world.

In 1957, The European Union was formed and has gained over twenty-five nations. They have now come up with their own currency call the Euro. They would like to see all the other nations adopt this type currency.

All of these nations believe in a new world order and are searching for the right person who will be a leader for this cause. Many names have come up, but so far no one has been elected as a permanent president or leader. In the near future, I believe that they will find just this leader when the Antichrist comes on the scene and will become this world leader.

In The United States of America, in the year 1979 an agency

came into being called FEMA, which stands for the Federal Emergency Management Agency. It was not voted on by congress, but was a product of a Presidential Executive Order.

The rules that this document carries are alarming. If FEMA became enacted by the President all kind of rules would take place on our rights as an American Citizen. The government would have the right to seize all communications media in the United States, the right to seize all means of transportation, the right to seize all airports and aircraft, the right to seize jobs of the American people and transfer anyone to any place to work and seize all means of travel from anyone the government chooses.

The amazing thing about the prospect of having a new world order is knowing the leaders who have endorsed this plan. Some are as follows:

The Pope, Pres. George Bush, Sr., Nelson Rockefeller, Henry Kissinger, Pres. Harry Truman, Pres. Bill Clinton, Pres. Dwight Eisenhower, Pres. Jimmy Carter, Barry Goldwater, Pres. Abraham Lincoln, Pres. Gorbachev of Russia, Pres. Obama, Fidel Castro, Colin Powell, George Soros, Walter Cronkite, Woodrow Wilson and many more leaders around the world.

CHAPTER THREE

THE RAPTURE

The word rapture comes from the Greek word "harpazo" which means "caught up. The word rapture does not appear in the Bible, although most people when they are referring to Jesus coming in the clouds to take the believers to heaven use the word rapture. There are many references in the Bible about Jesus coming again. No one knows the time it will take place or all the details, but according to the Bible it will happen soon.

Many people refer to the rapture as the Second Coming of Jesus, but they are two different periods of time. When the rapture takes place, Jesus will not come to earth, but will call for the dead in Christ to meet Him in the air. When the Second Coming takes place will be after Armageddon He comes to earth to live and reign.

The most popular scripture about the rapture is found in 1st. Thes. 4:16-17.

For the Lord Himself will descend from heaven with a shout, with the voice of an archangel, and with the trumpet of God, and the dead in Christ will rise first. Then we who are alive and remain shall be caught up together with them in the clouds to meet the Lord in the air, and thus we shall always be with the Lord.

When a person dies, their soul and spirit go to heaven. The body remains on earth until the time comes when Jesus will come and receive the bodies to be united with their soul and spirit. The soul and spirit has been in the presence of Jesus from the day that they died. They are alive and well, but they do not have a glorified body until the soul, spirit and body are together.

Jesus said in John 14:3 "And if I go and prepare a place for you, I will come again, and receive you unto myself, that where I am, there yea may be also."

In the rest of this chapter we will be discussing topics like "When will the rapture take place? Who will be in the rapture? What will happen after the rapture takes place?

WHEN WILL THE RAPTURE TAKE PLACE?

The Bible tells us that no one knows the day or the hour when Christ will come again. People have talked about it and looked forward to it for hundreds of years, ever since Jesus ascended into heaven. Jesus tells us that we will know when the time is growing near. In the previous chapter, many prophecies are listed that tell us that we are living in the end times and that we can look to see Jesus at any time. In the time that we live in now, sometimes it is like a forest fire is burning, you cannot see the flames, but you can see the smoke and know that the fire is fast approaching. Jesus told His disciples, when they asked Him when would the end come, He replied that no one knows, only the Father.

A lot of people have predicted certain dates when Jesus would come again. In 1987 a book was written called "88 Reasons that Jesus will come in 1988." The writer tries to connect scripture with his writings and a lot of people really began to believe him. When 1988 came and Jesus had not come, he said that he had miscalculated the date and that it would be later. One thing in his favor was that he sold a lot of books.

Others have claimed they have seen Jesus in different places and some have claimed that He was walking down the road and they picked him up and He rode with them for a while and suddenly disappeared.

When a person does not study and read the Bible, they will fall for almost any kind of nonsense that is going around the world today. Even some Christians will be caught up in a lot of things that does not line up with the Word of God and later wind up following some kind of cult.

HAS A RAPTURE TAKEN PLACE BEFORE?

They are at least four different places in the Bible where a rapture has taken place. The first one recorded was when Enoch was caught up and was seen no more.

ENOCH --Genesis 5:24. And Enoch walked with God; and he was not; for God took him.

Hebrews 11:5. By faith Enoch was translated that he should not see death, and was not found, because God had translated him; for his translation he had this testimony, that he pleased God.

Jude 1:14. And Enoch also, the seventh from Adam, prophesied of these, saying, Behold, the Lord cometh with ten thousands of his saints.

Enoch was three hundred years old when God took him. He was as close to living a perfect life as anyone who ever lived. According the Book of Jude, he probably was a prophet. There is a book called "The Book of Enoch" that is very interesting and tells the life of Enoch. He tells of things that existed on earth before the flood and of having talked with God and His angels. No one knows if this book authentic or not. If it is, there is a lot of valuable information in it.

ELIJAH-- 2 Kings 2:11. And it came to pass, as they still went on, and talked, that, behold there appeared a chariot of fire, and horses of fire, and parted them both asunder; and Elijah went up by a whirlwind into heaven.

The second rapture took place when Elijah was taken up in a whirlwind when the horses and chariots of fire appeared.

JESUS -- Acts 1:9 And when he had spoken these things, while they beheld, he was taken up: and a cloud received him out of their sight.

After being crucified, Jesus arose on the third day and for a period of forty days he met with his disciples each week and his last appearance was on Mount olivet. There he gave his last instructions to them and slowly ascended into the clouds out of their sight. There was four hundred witnesses watching him as he ascended to heaven.

SAINTS - Matthew 27:51-53. And behold, the veil of the temple was rent in twain from the top to the bottom; and the earth did quake, and the rocks rent; and the graves were opened; and many bodies of the saints which slept arose. And came out of the graves after his resurrection, and went into the holy city, and appeared unto many.

I suppose you could call this a resurrection and a rapture. The graves were opened and saints who had died were seen walking around. This is a scripture that is rarely preached on by today's ministers. The scripture never says what happened to the saints after they were seen walking and going into the holy city. But there is a scripture that I believe is connected to this incident. It is found in Ephesians 4:8-10 - When He ascended on high, He led captivity captive, and gave gifts to men. (Now this, "He ascended"--what does it mean but that He also first descended into the lower parts of the earth? He who descended is also the One who ascended far above all the heavens, that He might fill all things.)

I personally believe that after Jesus was crucified that he descended into Hades where the Saints and the lost were found. There were originally two sections, one was made up of the saints who were in Abraham's bosom, and the other located across a great gulf fixed between them where the lost were found living in torment. The scripture says that when " He ascended on high, He led captivity captive". I believe that he carried every saint from the day of creation up until the day of His crucifixion to a place called paradise located in heaven. When the thief was on a cross beside Jesus and he asked him to remember him, Jesus replied " Verily I say unto thee, Today shalt thou be with me in paradise." (Luke

23:43) I believe that this was the last rapture that has taken place until Jesus comes again.

There are a lot of scriptures that point to the rapture of Christians. The most quoted is found in 1st. Thessalonians 4:6. For the Lord himself shall descend from heaven with a shout, with the voice of the archangel, and with the trump of God: and the dead in Christ shall rise first: Then we which are alive and remain shall be caught up together with them in the clouds, to meet the Lord in the air, and so shall we ever be with the Lord.

This is when Jesus descends from heaven with a laud voice and the trump of God and calls for the dead in Christ to rise and meet Him in the air. Then the believers who are living at that time will rise to meet him also. There will no one left on the earth but unbelievers. This will be the greatest worldwide event that has ever happened during the history of mankind.

1 CORINTHIANS 15:50-53 - Now this I say, brethren, that flesh and blood cannot inherit the kingdom of God; neither doth corruption inherit incorruption. Behold, I show you a mystery; We shall not all sleep, but we shall all be changed in the twinkling of an eye, at the last trump; for the trumpet shall sound, and the dead shall be raised incorruptible, and we shall be changed.

It will be an exciting time when the dead and the living will have a brand new glorified body that is perfect in every way. The blind will see, the lame will walk, the feeble will be full of energy, all infirmities in our body will be gone and most of all we will be like Jesus.

Some believe that this is a secret rapture and the ones left behind will just be puzzled as to where everyone is gone. This can't be because of the devastation left behind after all the believers are gone. More details to this event are found later on in this chapter.

2 THESSALONIANS 2:3-4. Let no man deceive you by any means: for that day shall not come, except there come a falling away first, and that man of sin be revealed, the son of perdition; who opposeth and exalteth himself above all that is call God, or

that is worshipped; so that he as God sitteth in the temple of God, showing himself that he is God.

There has been a lot of different opinions pertaining to the part of the verse above that states "except there come a falling away first." Some believe that the falling away means that apostasy will take place and Satan will lead the world to follow him. Others believe that the falling away means the catching up of believers as in the rapture before Jesus comes again during the battle of Armageddon. In the Greek word used here is apostosia or depart from. This is a gray area like so many other places in the scripture where there is left somewhat of a question for men to study and discuss. One day we will know for certain what all the scripture means when it is explained by Jesus.

Paul is speaking of the Second Coming of Jesus when He returns to earth with all the saints who ever lived where they will reign with him for one thousand years and later for all eternity.

MATTHEW 24:40-41. Then shall two be in the field; the one shall be taken, and the other left. Two women shall be grinding at the mill; the one shall be taken, and the other left.

This is an example of what will be happening all around the world. Some will be taken in daytime and others will be sleeping at night. I believe that unbelievers will actually see their Christian love ones ascend into the clouds to meet Jesus just as he ascended before the people on Mount Olivet.

REVELATION 1:7. Behold, he cometh with clouds: and every eye shall see him, and all kindreds of the earth shall wail because of him. Even so, Amen.

When the rapture occurs and all of the Christians are taken out, it will literally mean that the true church will no longer exist. The Holy Spirit who dwells in the heart of every believer will naturally go with them. A lot of people believe that the Holy Spirit will no longer be on earth after the saints are gone, but this cannot be true because people will still be saved after the rapture and during the tribulation. God's word tells us that no man can come unto Jesus unless the Spirit draws him, so He would have to be present after the rapture.

After the rapture, this world as we know it will be changed completely. When you take all the Christians out at one time this will make a vast difference in world at that time.

2 THESSALONIANS 2:7. For the mystery of iniquity doth already work; only he who now letteth will let, until he be taken out of the way.

There is a lot of talk and discussion about the rapture and the connection with the great tribulation. Some say the rapture will take place before the tribulation which is called pre-tribulation. Others hold the belief that the rapture will take place during the middle of the tribulation which is called mid-tribulation belief. Some say that the rapture will take place after the tribulation is over.

When you read in the Bible about how God told Noah to build the ark and that He was going to destroy the world with water and bring His wrath upon the all living things on the earth, He told Noah that he and his family would be saved from His wrath. Noah and his family entered the ark and was safe during God's wrath.

When angels approached Lot while he and his family were living in the city of Sodom, they told him to take his family and leave the city because it would be destroyed. Lot did as the angels told him to do and they left the city before it was destroyed by fire and brimstone.

Just as he delivered Noah and Lot and their families I believe that God will deliver his church from his wrath. God allows man to go through tribulation caused by man, but when he uses his wrath as he will during the great tribulation, he allows his true children a way to escape. That is why I believe the saints will be removed from the earth before he begins to pour out his wrath by his judgments written in the Book of Revelation.

REVELATION 3:10. Because thou hast kept the word of my patience, I also will keep thee from the hour of temptation, which shall come upon all the world, to try them that dwell upon the earth.

Other scriptures that lead us to believe that the church will not go through the tribulation and the wrath of God are:

1 THES. 5:9, ROMANS 5:9, 2 PETER 2:9, 1 THES. 1:10, JOEL 2:28-31, MAL. 4:2, ZEP. 1:14-18, LUKE 21:36.

THE EARTH AFTER THE RAPTURE

When the rapture takes place, it will not be as some movies lead people to believe. They show people finding clothes laying on the floor of someone that is missing and just can't figure out what has happened to so many people that can't be found anywhere. This will be a time of devastation that never has been seen before. Many countries will not be affected as bad as others. Countries that worship idols and other Gods will be business as usual.

Nations that are considered as having many people who profess Christ as their Savior will be affected most. Can you imagine how many planes that are in the air over the United States? It estimated that over 5000 planes are in the air at one time over the U.S. In some estimations of how many true Christians that live in the United States, it is believed that only one out of every four people are true Christians. Using that figure this would mean that at the time of the rapture there would be over 1000 planes that would not have a pilot to land them because they would have been taken up to meet the Lord. With an average of 200 people on board, this would mean that 200,000 passengers would crash to the earth in the planes. Many flight controllers at the airports would be taken away leaving pilots to try to land on their own. This would be just a picture of U.S., not counting the rest of the world.

Can you also imagine during the daylight hours how many million cars are on the highways just in the U.S. and the thought of one out of four of those cars crashing into other cars. This could lead to thousands of deaths on the highways. Traffic in the cities would come to a grinding halt with hardly any way to get to homes.

Doctors performing operations at hospitals would suddenly vanish leaving patients on the operating tables. Store owners would be taken up leaving everything for looters to steal. Food would be stolen out of the stores, drugs stolen from the pharmacies. Prisons would be out of control with so many guards gone. Fire fighters could hardly control fires that have started.

When you have the remaining population left on earth made up of unsaved people there is no way to even imagine what will be going on. Rather some people believe it or not, when the church made up of believers is taken out of the way, what used to be Christian nations will suffer most because of so many people being absent and have to start the clean up process and getting things to running again. I believe that the U.S. will be affected the most by the absence of so many people and other world powers will take advantage of the situation and could probably lose the status of being the most powerful nation on earth.

After days and weeks of frustration after the rapture, some people will come to realize what has happened and remember Christians witnessing to them and ask Jesus to come into their heart. Others who realize that they were just playing church and had not really been saved, now turns to Jesus. This will be a hard life to live as a Christian, having to take a lot of the scorn and abuse that will come from unbelievers even before the Antichrist comes on the scene.

When thousands of people who are left behind start to reading Bibles that are left in churches and homes learn that seven years after the Antichrist signs a peace pact with many nations, that Jesus will come again to earth and defeat all the enemies of God. Even the enemies will know the exact date he will return and even try to stand and fight the armies of God.

A lot of people have been taught by some of the leading Bible Scholars that the seven year tribulation will start the day after the rapture takes place. Nowhere in the scripture does it say this. The tribulation could be one year, ten years or even fifty years from the time of the rapture. The Bible tells us that when the Antichrist comes on the scene and proclaims a seven year peace treaty with Israel that the seventh week spoken of by Daniel will start called "the great tribulation."

DANIEL 9:27. And he (the Antichrist) shall confirm the covenant with many for one week: and in the midst of the week he shall cause the sacrifice and the oblation to cease and for the overspreading of abominations he shall make it desolate, even until the consummation, and that determined shall be poured upon the desolate.

No matter how much a person trusts or believes a pastor, a friend, a writer or a famous scholar, always go to the Bible to confirm what a person has said. To do otherwise is a risky situation.

How many times have you heard someone make a statement and say that it is in the Bible, when you try to find it, it is not there. A lot of old sayings that have been repeated down through the years that someone will say that it came from the Bible, but it did not.

SOUL SLEEP

Some denominations teach that when a person dies that his soul stays in the grave until Jesus comes again. They ask the question " How can Jesus bring the saints with their soul and spirit back with him during the rapture when their soul suppose to be still in the grave?" They use a verse of scripture from the Book of Ecclesiastes 9:5 to try to prove their point, which is " For the living know that they will die: but the dead know nothing, and they have no more reward, for the memory of them is forgotten." This statement is speaking of the dead body. The dead body surely does not know anything for the soul and spirit are gone on to either heaven or hell.

One main scripture that disproves the idea of soul sleep is found in Luke 16:19-31 where Lazarus and the rich man have both died, but their souls and spirits are still alive. They talk to one another, they see each other and the rich man who is in the side of

Hades where the lost are at makes the statement that he was tormented in a flame of fire. They are alive and are able to see, feel, talk and hear each other.

Other scriptures that disprove soul sleep are:

2 CORINTHIANS 5:6,8-9 Therefore we are always confident, knowing that, whilst we are at home in the body, we are absent from the lord....We are confident, I say, and willing rather to be absent from the body, and to be present with the Lord. Wherefore we labor, that, whether present or absent, we may be accepted of him.

ECCLESIASTES 12:7 Then the dust return to the earth as it was: and the spirit shall return to God who gave it.

MATTHEW 17:13-4 And after six days Jesus taketh Peter, James and John his brother, and bringeth them up into an high mountain apart and was transfigured before them, and his face did shine as the sun, and his raiment was white as the light. And behold, there appeared unto them Moses and Elias talking with him.

These verses prove that when we die, our soul and spirit go to be with the Lord or to Hades. Those who go to heaven will one day come in the clouds with Jesus to meet their bodies in the air and return to heaven. Those who go to Hades will linger in torment for at least one thousand years while the millennium takes place and after that they will be judged at the great white throne judgment.

CHAPTER FOUR

THE WAR WITH GOG AND MAGOG

In the Book of Ezekiel, chapters 38 and 39, it tells of a time when several nations will attack the nation of Israel.

EZEKIEL 38:1-6 And The word of the Lord came unto, saying, Son of man, set thy face against Gog, the land of Magog, the chief prince of Meshech and Tubal, and prophesy against him. And say, Thus saith the Lord God; Behold, I am against thee, O Gog, the chief prince of Meshech and Tubal; And I will turn thee back, and put hooks into thy jaws, and I will bring thee forth, and all thine army, horses and horsemen, all of them clothed with all sorts of armor, even a great company with bucklers and shields, all of them handling swords; Persia, Ethiopia and Libya with them; all of them with shield and helmet; Gomer, and all his bands; the house of Togarmah of the north quarters, and all his bands; and many people with thee.

The word of the Lord came to Ezekiel and told him of a great war that would happen sometime in the future against Israel. He told him that He would put hooks in their jaws or put an idea in their minds that they could go against Israel and defeat the entire nation.

There have been a lot of different definitions about the names of some of the leaders and nations who will be leading in this attack. The word "Gog" is agreed by many to be a leader or king of a nation or nations that will lead the attack on the land of Israel.

WHAT NATIONS WILL BE INVOLVED?

MAGOG - A lot of prophecy teachers agree that this land is probably Russia.
ROSH - This could be a part of Russia or Central Asia.
MESHECH - Part of Russia or Turkey
TUBAL - Part of Russia or Turkey

PERSIA - This would be present day Iran whose name was changed from Persia to Iran in 1935.
ETHIOPIA - Sudan
GOMER - Turkey

It seems that the country of Russia is the only one that is not of the nation of Islam in this war. This would be the largest gathering of Muslims to attack Israel since the six day war of 1967, when Israel beat them in less than a week.

WHEN WILL THIS WAR TAKE PLACE?

We know that it will take place at a time when Israel will be living in peace and security.

EZEKIEL 38:11 And thou shalt say, I will go up to the land of unwalled villages; I will go to them that are at rest, that dwell safely, all of them dwelling without walls, and having neither bars nor gates.

We know that at the present time there is unrest in Israel. We also know that for many years there has not been any walls or gates in the cities of Israel.

Some believe that all of this will take place during the great tribulation. This would be somewhat unlikely, because this would be when the Antichrist is in control of the whole world and would not be just a leader of a few countries.

Some even believe that this battle is talking about the battle of Armageddon. Some things that happen at this time are similar in

Chapter Four: The War with Gog and Magog

detail such as earthquakes, fire, brimstone and hail. The main difference in this war and the battle of Armageddon is that the Bible says that "all the nations of the earth will gather" against Jerusalem, not just a few nations, for the final battle and no one will be left alive who comes against God

I believe that this battle will take place sometime after the rapture of the Church.

One reason is that the United States has been an ally of Israel for many years and other countries of the world know that if anyone declared all out war with Israel that the USA would come to their rescue.

When the rapture of the church takes place, Christians from all over the world will be caught up to meet Jesus in the air. The world has over six billion people now and probably over eighty per cent are made up of Muslims, Hindus, Buddhists, atheists and unbelievers who will be left behind. The United States is a Christian Nation and would probably have more believers taken up than any other nation.

After all the turmoil that would be left behind after the rapture and the nation as a whole with no Christians left this nation would be at the mercy of other nations of the world, because a lot of them would have so few taken up, there would be very little difference in the unbelieving countries and there would be just business as usual. With no believers living in the U. S. after the rapture, I would think that there would be no one who would want to protect or help support Israel any longer. This would be a perfect time for someone like Magog and the other nations to try to defeat Israel.

Another theory is that there will be a series of EMP Bombs will be detonated all over the world.

What is the EMP Bomb?

The EMP Bomb (electromagnetic pulse bomb) is a bomb that has finally been successfully made by several countries including the United States of America. This bomb is made up of electromagnetic pulse devices that when exploded over a city like Omaha, Nebraska, could wipe out all electrical operations over the entire nation. A bomb of this nature is designed to completely destroy the operations of all electrical systems used at the time it explodes. We are told that when it explodes that it would be similar to a flash of lightning and the damage would be done just that fast, although this device will not harm humans or buildings.

All devices using copper wire such as cars, airplanes, computers, radios, all electrical grids across the nation, electricity in homes and stores, satellites and appliances would become completely useless. This is a no repair situation after this device exploded. Can you imagine in less than a second the whole nation could be thrown back 200 years, when no electricity existed?

We are told that this device can be built for only $400.00 after the formula has been acquired. Several nations, such as Iran and North Korea, are working on this device and will probably have it within a year. When they acquire it, they will be the biggest threat to the world that has ever been.

It seems to be just a matter of time until all nations will have access to this devastating bomb. Can you imagine when the first EMP bomb is exploded, a chain reaction of all the countries who have one, one country after the other will be attacking another and in a few days the whole world will be completely void of any electricity.

Food supplies all over the world would soon be used up. People would have to start tilling the soil by mule and plow for there would be no tractors running because the fuel would have been used up and there will be no way to produce any more for the refineries would not be running because of situation that has been left by the EMP bomb. This would be a time of turmoil with people starving and no way for a quick fix to this vast problem.

The only way of any country attacking another would be by ground troops. Planes would be useless. All communications would be down. Ammunition for guns would soon run out with no way to

Chapter Four: The War with Gog and Magog | 49

produce any more.

Can you imagine going from the high tech armies of today to having to use primitive weapons like bows and arrows, spears and swords? This would be a time in history when the nation with the most people would dominate during a time of war.

EZEKIEL 38: 4 - And I will turn thee back and put hooks into thy jaws, and I will bring thee forth, and all thine army, horses and horsemen, all of them clothed with all sorts of Armor, even a great company with bucklers and shields, all of them handling swords.

EZEKIEL 38:15 - And thou shalt come from thy place out of the north parts, thou, and many people with thee, all of them riding upon horses, a great company, and a mighty army.

This is a description of the war on Israel by Gog and Magog. They are using primitive weapons to use in this attack. Some would say that this is not literally speaking of older weapons being used in this war. They say that Ezekiel is speaking symbolic because he could not describe modern weapons of war. Most of the time in scripture when it is not clear about what the writer is describing, they will use a phrase for example: Rev. 8:8 And the second angel sounded, and as it were a great mountain burning with fire was cast into the sea; and the third part of the sea became blood. John says "as it were a great mountain burning with fire". He just described it as best he could. Ezekiel wrote the word of prophecy exactly as it was given to him by God. I believe that He is literally talking about ground troops using horses and weapons like those that were used centuries ago. The country of Russia at present time has more horses than any country in the world. They could easily share them with their allies from the Islamic countries to help fight against Israel.

EZEKIEL 38:9-12 Thou shalt ascend and come like a storm, thou shalt be like a cloud to cover the land, thou, and all thy bands, and many people with thee. Thus saith the Lord God; It shall also come to pass, that at the same time shall things come into thy mind, and thou shalt think an evil thought: And thou shalt say, I will go up to the land of unwalled villages; I will go to them that are at rest, that dwell safely, all of them dwelling without walls, and having neither bars nor gates, to take a spoil, and to take a prey; to turn thine hand upon the desolate places that are now inhabited, and upon the people that are gathered out of the nations, which have gotten cattle and goods, that dwell in the midst of the land.

EZEKIEL 38:15-16 - And thou shalt come from thy place out of the north parts, thou, them riding upon horses, a great company, and a mighty army; And thou shalt come up against my people of Israel, as a cloud to cover the land; it shall be in the latter days, and I will bring thee against my land, and that the heathen may know me, when I shall be sanctified in thee, O Gog, before their eyes.

Gog, the chief prince of Magog, Meshech and Tubal will be convinced that the small country of Israel cannot withstand all of the hundreds of thousands that he leads and will attempt to crush Israel. This will be unlike the modern day Israel, that has the best military for it's size in existence today. If ground troops were not to be used at this time, why wouldn't Russia and all of their allies just use modern day aircraft and destroy Israel, after all they out number Israel about two hundred million to about seven million?

WHY THE INVASION ON ISRAEL?

The land of Israel has been the envy of a lot of nations around the world because of its vast resources in the Dead Sea. It contains 45 billion tons of sodium, chlorine, sulfur, potassium, calcium, magnesium and bromide. This would be reason enough for Russia to make war with Israel.

All the Muslim nations would gladly help Russia just to destroy the land of Israel. They have such a hatred of the Jews that has been going on for hundreds of years. They have tried to destroy Israel many times in the last fifty years, but has always been unsuccessful.

GOD'S PURPOSE FOR THE INVASION

EZEKIEL 38:18-19, 23 - And it shall come to pass at the same time when Gog shall come against the land of Israel, saith the Lord God, that my fury shall come up in my face. For in my jealousy and in the fire of my wrath have I spoken, Surely in that day there shall be a great shaking in the land of Israel; Thus will I magnify myself, and sanctify myself; and I will be known in the eyes of many nations, and they shall know that I am the Lord.

I believe the last verse sums it up as the reason that God is against Gog. He says "and they shall know that I am the Lord." This statement is repeated in four different verses in Ezekiel chapters 38 and 39 to clearly indicate that this is the main reason for pouring out His wrath on this invading armies. At this point in time God has allowed all these countries over a long period of time to do everything that they can to destroy Israel, but still have not had victory. I believe that all these nations have served other gods until God has had enough and will literally show them that He is the only true God of the universe. He will lead them into a place where He will show them through His wrath that He is the only God.

EZEKIEL 38:20-22 - So that the fishes of the sea, and the fowls of the heaven, and the beasts of the field, and all creeping things that creep upon the earth, and the earth, shall shake at my presence, and the mountains shall be thrown down, and the steep places shall fall, and every wall shall fall to the ground. And I will call for a sword against him throughout all my mountains, saith the Lord God: every man's sword shall be against his brother. And I will plead against him with pestilence and with blood; and I will rain upon him, and upon his bands, and upon the many people that are with him an overflowing rain, and great hailstones, fire, and brimstone.

This will be a time when God pours out his wrath upon the enemy of Israel in full force. This will be a preview of the battle of Armageddon. When they arrive on the mountains of Israel He will shake the earth like never before with earthquakes, overflowing rain, great hailstones, fire and brimstone. He will bring delusions among the enemy and they will even start to fight each other, just as it happened at times in the battles of the Old Testament. This will be a battle like the world has never seen before. It will be over in a short while and the number of the dead will amount to five out of every six of the whole army from the North.

EZEKIEL 39:2 - And I will turn thee back and leave but the sixth part of thee, and will cause thee to come up from the north parts, and will bring thee upon the mountains of Israel.

There will be so many dead until God will call upon ravenous birds of every sort and to the beasts of the field to devour the bodies. It will take seven months for Israel to bury the bodies. Men will be employed just to look for the remains of these dead bodies.

EZEKIEL 38:12 - And seven months shall the house of Israel be burying of them, that they may cleans the land.

Then another proof that primitive weapons will be used is the verse below.

EZEKIEL 38:9 - And they that dwell in the cities of Israel shall go forth, and shall set on fire and burn the weapons, both the shields and the bucklers, the bows and the arrows, and the hand staves, and the spears, and they shall burn them with fire seven years.

The present day weapons consist of rifles, grenades, rocket launchers, tanks and many other type weapons that are made of some type steel. None of these weapons could be used in building fires. When you read Ezekiel, chapters 38 and 39, it reminds you of movies that you have seen that are made after a world has been demolished by wars and hardly anyone survives with hardly any weapons left and they struggle to survive. There will be a scene like this in the land of the invading countries especially Russia, for God will pour out his wrath of fire on them.

EZEKIEL 38: 6 - And I will send a fire on Magog, and among them that dwell carelessly in the isles: and they shall know that I am the Lord.

A lot of times when a catastrophe of great magnitude happens when hurricanes, tornadoes, storms and earthquakes hit countries people say that God is pouring out His wrath. This is not quite correct. When God pours out His wrath He has a specific reason for doing so. Reasons, such as, the flood in Noah's day because of the unrighteous acts of men on the earth at that time. Another is completely destroying Sodom and Gomorrah when there were no righteous people living there except Lot, his two daughters and his wife.

Many actions that have taken place in modern wars have been called an act of God incorrectly, such as the atomic bomb used on Japan during World War Two. Acts such as these are manmade and are not the wrath of God. Some are convinced that a lot of the horrible acts that happen in the Book of Revelation are done by man, such as fire coming down from heaven, earthquakes and other catastrophes are a series of atomic bombs. I am convinced that when God opens the seals, the trumpets and the viles man will truly know that this is the true wrath of God.

After the dusts settles from the war with Gog and Magog, God tells His people that He will no longer hide His face from the House of Israel but will continue to bless them.

EZEKIEL 39:29 - Neither will I hide my face any more from them, for I have poured out my spirit upon the house of Israel, saith the Lord God.

CHAPTER FIVE

THE ANTICHRIST

The word "anti" means "against" or the "opposite of something". The word antichrist literally means "against Christ or against God." The word "antichrist" is found only four times in the Bible.

1 JOHN 2:18-19 Little children, it is the last time; and as you have heard that antichrist shall come, even now are there many antichrists; whereby we know that it is the last time. They went out from us, but they were not of us: for if they had been of us, they would no doubt have continued with us: but they went out, that they might be made manifest that they were not all of us.

1 JOHN 2:22-23 Who is a liar but he that denieth that Jesus is the Christ? He is antichrist, that denieth the Father and the Son. Whosoever denieth the Son, the same hath not the Father; but he that acknowledgeth the Son hath the Father also.

1 JOHN 4:2-3 Hereby know ye the Spirit of God: Every spirit that confesseth that Jesus Christ is come in the flesh is of God: And every spirit that confesseth not that Jesus Christ is come in the flesh is not of God: and this is that spirit of antichrist, whereof ye have heard that it should come; and even now already is it in the world.

2 JOHN 1:7 For many deceivers are entered into the world, who confess not that Jesus Christ is come in the flesh, This is a deceiver and an antichrist.

Just as the apostle John spoke in his epistles of antichrists in the time he was living, there are many antichrists in the world today. In the news each day we hear someone trying to degrade the name of Jesus. It is a common thing for people to come against anyone who professes to be a Christian and is trying to promote the Gospel of Jesus to be slandered and talked about. They use the phrase "freedom of speech" to justify their actions. People like these are surely antichrists, but there is coming a day when a man will come out of the world population who will become the one spoken of in the Book of Daniel and Revelation. He will be called "The Antichrist" and will someday rule the world.

He is mentioned in the book of Revelation for the first time a "beast. Rev. 13:1 And I stood upon the sand of the sea, and saw a beast rise up out of the sea, having seven heads and ten horns, and upon his horns ten crowns, and upon his heads the name of blasphemy.

Sometime after the rapture has taken place, which could be the next year or even fifty years later, a man will appear on the world scene that will eventually have control of the whole world. Some prophecy writers tend to believe that the day after the rapture takes place that the Antichrist comes on the scene and the seven years of tribulation will begin. Nowhere in the Bible is this taught. The Bible tells us that the Antichrist will make a peace treaty with Israel and the rest of the world and the seven years of tribulation will begin according to the Book of Daniel.

DANIEL 9:27 And he shall confirm the covenant with many for one week; and in the midst of the week he shall cause the sacrifice and the oblation to cease, and for the overspreading of abominations he shall make it desolate, even until the consummation, and that determined shall be poured upon the desolate.

After the rapture of the church, the world will be in such turmoil that it could take years for it to become normal again. During this time the Antichrist will be making his move to become a savior to the world and gain control of it through his leadership.

WHO IS THE ANTICHRIST?

For years people have been trying to identify who the antichrist is. They have picked world leaders who have died and those who are living. They have tried to take their names and combine them with the numbers 666 who the antichrist will use to control people in the Book of Revelation. Some have been dead for hundreds of years and others who are still living. They believe that some way those who are dead will come back to life to become the Antichrist. Some names thought about are:

- Adolph Hitler
- Joseph Stalin
- Antiochus Epiphanes
- Nero - Roman Emperor
- Napoleon
- Franklin D. Roosevelt
- John F. Kennedy
- Henry Kissinger
- Bill Gates
- Barrack Obama

Everybody likes to speculate and make a guess who the Antichrist might be. No one knows who he is. He could be living at this present time or it could be years before he is even born.

WHERE WILL HE COME FROM?

After the death of Alexander the Great, his four generals divided his empire and assumed control of different countries. Lysimachus received Thrace and most of Asia Minor. Cassander obtained Macedonia and Greece. Ptolemy was given Egypt, Palestine, Cilicia, Petra, and Cyprus. Seleucus controlled the rest of Asia, Syria, Babylon, Persia, and India.

A lot of scholars believe that the Antichrist will come out of one of these countries.

DANIEL 8:9 And out of one of them came forth a little horn, which waxed exceeding great, toward the south, and toward the east, and toward the pleasant land.

The Antichrist will be the little horn that will come out of the revived Roman Empire which will have ten kings and he will pluck three of them up by the roots.

DANIEL 7:8 I considered the horns, and, behold, there came up among them another little horn, before whom there were three of the first horns plucked up by the roots; and, behold, in this horn were eyes like the eyes of man, and a mouth speaking great things.

If this be true then he would come out of Lebanon or Syria.

Some think that he will be a Jew, because of the way that he will be trusted in the beginning and will bring about a peace treaty to last for seven years. Others say this would not be possible because with over one billion Muslims around the world he would not be accepted.

WHAT WILL HE BE LIKE?

According to the scriptures in the Bible, he will come on the world scene like no one has ever seen before. He will be someone who will be accepted by all the nations of the earth as a magnificent leader. He will have occasion to have brought peace to countries and will become like a savior to them and they would die for him if need be. He will be accepted by the Jews as if he was the Messiah that they have been waiting for. Some of the things that he will do and be involved in are written in the scriptures below:

DANIEL 7:23-24 And the ten horns out of this kingdom are ten kings that shall arise and another shall rise after them; and he shall be diverse from the first, and he shall subdue three kings, and the ten horns out of this kingdom are ten kings that shall arise and another shall rise after them; and he shall be diverse from the first, and he shall subdue three kings.

The revived Roman Empire is already in existence today. They are members of the European Union. In 1957 six countries signed the Treaties of Rome which would later become known as the European Union. They were Belgium, France, Italy, Luxembourg, the Netherlands, and West Germany. In 1973 three more joined, which were Denmark, Ireland and the United Kingdom. To date they are 27 countries that make up the European Union.

When the Antichrist rises to power he will in some way defeat three of the ten kingdoms and take over the rest of the countries and have control of them as it says in Daniel, Chapter 7.

THE RIDER ON THE WHITE HORSE

REVELATION 6:2 And I saw, and behold a white horse: and he that sat on him had a bow, and a crown was given unto him: and he went forth conquering, and to conquer.

To the world the Antichrist will appear as a rider on a white horse who will act as a modern day Robin Hood. He will conquer the bad and rescue the down trodden. In this verse you will notice that no arrows are mentioned with bow that he is carrying. This is why he is believed to be able to literally talk to the leaders of the countries and get them to believe a lie and surrender or join forces with him without waging an all out war.

Some think that the headquarters of the Antichrist will be in the United Nations Building in New York. On the outside of this building is a statue of someone riding a horse carrying a bow with no arrows. Could this be just a coincidence or could it be related to prophecy of the rider on the white horse?

HE WILL CORRUPT BY FLATTERIES

DANIEL ll:21 And in his estate shall stand up a vile person, to whom they shall not give the honor of the kingdom; but he shall come in peaceably, and obtain the kingdom by flatteries.

He will be a man who will come in peace and use the method of flattery on the leaders of other countries until they begin to trust him and join in with him in all the plans that he has to offer. He will be like farmer who wants to lead an animal into a pen for slaughter when he uses corn or other pieces of food to lead them into a pen where there is no escape

HE WILL SPEAK WORDS AGAINST GOD

DANIEL 7:25 And he shall speak great words against the most High, and shall wear out the saints of the most High, and think to change times and laws; and they shall be given into his hand until a time and times and the dividing.

DANIEL 7:36 And the king shall do according to his will; and he shall exalt himself, and magnify himself above every god, and shall speak marvelous things against the God of gods, and shall prosper till the indignation be accomplished; for that that is determined shall be done.

MATTHEW 24:15 When ye therefore shall see the abomination of desolation, spoken of by Daniel the prophet, stand in the holy place, (whoso readeth, let him understand);

2 THESSALONIANS 2:4 Who opposeth and exalteth himself above all that is called God, or that is worshipped; so that he as God sitteth in the temple of God, showing himself that he is God.

He will blaspheme God and set up his own laws for men to follow instead of laws that were given by God to follow. He will be a world dictator like no one has ever seen before. He will change from the peacemaker that everyone believed he was, and for the last three and one half years of the tribulation he will be possessed by Satan and actually believe that he is God.

HE WILL DISREGARD THE WORD OF HIS FATHERS

DANIEL 11:37 Neither shall he regard the God of his fathers, nor the desire of women, nor regard any god: for he shall magnify himself above all.

This verse is used by a lot of people who believe that he will be a Jew. This is a term that is normally used by Jews in referring to their ancestors. The only question about him being a Jew would be, how would he be accepted by the Islamic nations? The situation today between the Muslims and the Jews is not well at all, so the world leader would have to literally work a miracle to be accepted by the Muslims.

Some believe that he will also be a homosexual because of not having the desire for women. This could be or he could be so intent on being a kind of god until he would not have time to become involved with women.

HE WILL RECEIVE A FATAL INJURY

REVELATION 13:3 And I saw one of his heads as it were wounded to death; and his deadly wound was healed: and all the world wondered after the beast.

For the first three and one half years after he brings about a peace treaty with Israel and the rest of the world, he rules the world as a dictator and does not seem to be a violent man. After three and one half years, he receives a wound to the head and apparently dies. Then something miraculous happens. He is healed and brought back to life. It seems that he becomes a completely new person with a desire to kill the saints of God and impose all kind of sanctions upon them. A lot of prophecy writers believe that this is the same time that Satan is thrown out of heaven and down to dwell on earth.

HE MAKES WAR WITH THE SAINTS

REVELATION 12:7-9 And there was war in heaven: Michael and his angels fought against the dragon; and the dragon fought and his angels, And prevailed not; neither was their place found any more in heaven; And the great dragon was cast out, that old serpent, called the Devil, and Satan which deceiveth the whole world: he was cast out into the earth, and his angels were cast out with him.

It appears that through his satanic power, Satan brings the Antichrist to life and then actually possesses his body and mind. From that moment on the Antichrist is like another person. Satan starts to control his every move and sets up a different lifestyle with a purpose to destroy the Christian people of that day.

REVELATION 13:6-7 And he opened his mouth in blasphemy against God, to blaspheme his name, and his tabernacle, and them that dwell in heaven. And it was given unto him to make war with the saints, and to overcome them; and power was given him over all kindreds, and tongues, and nations.

HE WILL STOP THE DAILY SACRIFICES

DANIEL 8:12 And an host was given him against the daily sacrifice by reason of transgression, and it cast down the truth to the ground; and it practiced, and prospered.

DANIEL 11:31 And arms shall stand on his part, and they shall pollute the sanctuary of strength, and shall take away the daily sacrifice, and they shall place the abomination that maketh desolate.

DANIEL 12 And from the time that the daily sacrifice shall be taken away, and the abomination that maketh desolate set up, there shall be a thousand two hundred and ninety days.

The Antichrist under the control of Satan will immediately stop all sacrifices that the Jews had implemented after the new temple was built in Jerusalem. Sometime after the rapture occurs the new temple is built in Jerusalem and the Jews have returned to the routine of daily sacrifice as was their custom over two thousand years ago. He is determined to stop anything that has to do with the worship of God. From this point on he will stop anything that has to do with the worship of God by the Jews.

HE WILL SHOW SIGNS AND WONDERS

2 THESSALONIANS 2:9 Even him, whose coming is after the working of Satan with all power and signs and lying wonders.

2 THESSALONIANS 2:11 And for this cause God shall send them strong delusion, that they should believe a lie.

Many people will be fully convinced that he is actually a god when they see all of his power in action. When the people totally disregard the true God, He will send them strong delusion and just let them completely be caught up in the actions of the antichrist. They will believe all of the miracles that he performs and be as a young child when he sees a magic show and believes all of the tricks that the magician does.

NAMES OF THE ANTICHRIST

A lot of names has been given to the Antichrist in the old and new testament. Some of them are:

THE ANTICHRIST: 1 John 2:22 Who is a liar but the that denieth that Jesus is the Christ? He is antichrist, that denieth the Father and the Son.

BEAST: Revelation 17:8 "The beast that thou sawest was, and is not: and shall ascend out of the bottomless pit, and go into perdition: and they that dwell on the earth shall wonder, whose names were not written in the book of life from the foundation of the world, when they behold the beast that was, and is not, and yet is."

THE LITTLE HORN: Daniel 7:8 "I considered the horns, and behold, there came up among them another little horn, before whom there were three of the first horns plucked up by the roots: and, behold, in this horn were eyes like the eyes of man, and a mouth speaking great things."

THE MAN OF SIN: 2 Thessalonians 2:3 Let no man deceive you by any means: for that day shall not come, except there come a falling away first, and that man of sin be revealed, the son of perdition.

THE FALSE PROPHET

After the Antichrist is empowered by Satan, another person appears on the scene and will make the unholy trinity - Satan, Antichrist and the False Prophet.

REVELATION 13:11-14 And I beheld another beast coming up out of the earth; and he had two horns like a lamb, and he spake as a dragon. And he exerciseth all the power of the first beast before him, and causeth the earth and them which dwell therein to worship the first beast, whose deadly wound was healed. And he doeth great wonders, so that he maketh fire come down from heaven on the earth in the sight of men.

This beast that is called the False Prophet comes out of the earth, which is often referred to someone of the Jewish nationality, and becomes the next in power to the Antichrist. He is given power by Satan to perform all kinds of miracles including calling fire down from the sky. He even makes an image of the antichrist for everyone to worship and even causes it to speak.

REVELATION 13:13-15 And he doeth great wonders, so that he maketh fire come down from heaven on the earth in the sight of men. And deceiveth them that dwell on the earth by the means of those miracles which he had power to do in the sight of the beast; saying to them that dwell on the earth, that they should make an image to the beast, which had the wound by a sword, and did live. And he had power to give life unto the image of the beast, that the image of the beast should both speak and cause that as many as would not worship the image of the beast should be killed.

He will be given power by Satan to create some kind of image dedicated to the Antichrist similar to the image of Nebuchadnezzar in the book of Daniel.

DANIEL 3:1 Nebuchadnezzar the king made an image of gold, whose height was threescore cubits, and the breadth thereof six cubits: he set it up in the plain of Dura, in the Province of Babylon.

This was a image that was about 90 feet tall and 9 feet wide, which everyone was commanded to bow down and worship, and if they did not they would be cast into the fiery furnace and burned to death.

The False Prophet is thought by many to be a preacher or even the Pope himself at that period of time. By the name " false prophet", this would be in line with someone of a religious order. Some believe that he will be the leader of a worldwide religion during the time of the Antichrist. Some believe that he could be of the Muslim faith embracing the life of the Prophet Mohammed. At present time there are around one and one half billion Muslims in the world today.

THE BEAST AND FALSE PROPHET DESTROYED

After the battle of Armageddon, which is fought at the end of the seven year tribulation period, the Beast and the False Prophet are thrown into the lake of fire.

REVELATION 19:20 And the beast was taken, and with him the false prophet that wrought miracles before him, with which he deceived them that had received the mark of the beast, and them that worshipped his image. These both were cast alive into a lake of fire burning with brimstone.

CHAPTER SIX

THE GREAT TRIBULATION

THE BEGINNING

The apostle John writes the first three chapters in the book of Revelation to the seven churches in Asia. The revelation is given to him by Jesus Christ. He writes these letters in the present tense as the churches were active while he was living at that time. The rest of the book of Revelation is all in the future from that time on and the things that Jesus tells him start coming to pass around the 1900's and through the present day we are living in.

After chapter three is written, the church is not mentioned anymore, because all believers has been raptured and their souls are in heaven with Jesus

After writing these letters to the churches he is taken up in the spirit to heaven to be given a firsthand look at what will happen in the future.

REVELATION 4:1-2 After this I looked, and, behold, a door was opened in heaven: and the first voice which I heard was as it were of a trumpet talking with me; which said, come up hither; and I will shew thee things which must be hereafter. And immediately I was in the spirit: and, behold, a throne was set in heaven, and one sat on the throne

The apostle John was going to begin a journey to the future

that he had never dreamed of. He was going to actually see the things that Jesus told him of while he was on earth. The first thing he saw was a throne and someone sitting on it.

REVELATION 4:3 And he that sat was to look upon like a jasper and a sardine stone: and there was a rainbow round about the throne, in sight like unto an emerald.

John wrote what he saw as best he could describe. He knew that he was standing in the very presence of Almighty God sitting on his throne. There was a beauty that he could not describe only it resembled jasper and sardine stone with a rainbow around the throne that looked like an emerald. After seeing sight, he looked around and begins to see many other heavenly beings.

REVELATION 4:4-5 And round about the throne were four and twenty seats; and upon the seats I saw four and twenty elders sitting, clothed in white raiment; and they had on their heads crowns of gold. And out of the throne proceeded lightings and thundering and voices: and there were seven lamps of fire burning before the throne, which are the seven spirits of God.

John saw a group of twenty four people sitting around the throne clothed in white raiments. He does not say who they were, but many believe that they were the twelve apostles and twelve who represented the twelve tribes of Israel. They were all dressed in white apparel, which represents purity and someone who has been redeemed through the blood of Jesus. Some would say that if twelve of them were the apostles he would have recognized them and told who they were, especially if one of them was himself. Regardless of who they are, born again believers will know someday.

John describes other beings that he saw and what they were doing.

REVELATION 4:7-8 And before the throne there was a sea of glass like unto crystal: and in the midst of the throne, and round about the throne, were four beasts full of eyes before and behind. And the first beast was like a lion, and the second beast like a calf,

Chapter Six: The Great Tribulation | 69

and the third beast had a face as a man, and the fourth beast was like a flying eagle. And the four beasts had each of them six wings about him; and they were full of eyes within; and they rest not day and night, saying, Holy, holy, holy, Lord God Almighty, which was, and is, and is to come.

John was surely amazed at what he saw around the throne. As he looked at these beasts, he probably remembered reading in the writings of Ezekiel where he saw living creatures called Seraphims - angels of God.

EZEKIEL 5:6 Also out of the midst thereof came the likeness of four living creatures. And this was their appearance; they had the likeness of a man. And every one had four faces, and everyone had four wings.

These beings worshipped and praised God without ceasing day or night.

Another sight that had to be amazing to John was the number of heavenly host that surrounded the throne of God.

REVELATION 5:12 And I beheld, and I heard the voice of many angels round about the throne and the beast and the elders: and the number of them was ten thousand times ten thousand, and thousands of thousands.

John described the number of angels as best he could. Never had any earthly being ever witnessed the number that he saw. Some scholars have tried to figure exactly how many he was talking about and they can only say that John must have seen millions upon millions, if not billions. Just think, if every human being had one guardian angel to look after them, there would still be millions of angels left praising God in heaven.

At this time John sees the hand of God that has a book or scroll that is written on both sides and sealed with six seals. Jesus comes forward and takes the book from his hand.

REVELATION 5:1, 7 And I saw in the right hand of him that sat on the throne a book written within and on the backside, sealed with seven seals. And he came and took the book out of the right hand of him that sat upon the throne.

At this time Jesus opens the first seal of the book and many believe that this is the time that the Antichrist comes on the scene. The rapture has taken place and the world is in chaos. The battle of Gog and Magog against Israel is over and the world is looking for someone to lead the nations to peace and survival. The Antichrist will arise with a plan that can lead the world out of all the trouble that has taken place. He will lead the world through a one world government which begins with the revival of the countries from the old Roman Empire. He will be the leader of ten nations and will convince the world through his cunning ways and will literally brainwash all the other nations that he is the Messiah. Evan Israel will believe what he says when he presents them with a peace plan that they accept.

In Daniel, chapter 9, he tells about a time in the future when this man of sin will make his move. He states that there will be sixty-nine weeks (one week equals seven years) from the time that the temple of Jerusalem is beginning to be rebuilt after the return of the Jews from Babylon, until the Messiah is cut off, which was the crucifixion of Jesus.

NEHEMIAH 2:5-8 And I said unto the king, if it please the king, and if thy servants have found favour in thy sight, that thou wouldest send me unto Judah, unto the city of my fathers' sepulchers, that I may rebuild it. And the king said unto me, (the queen also sitting by him,) For how long shall thy journey be? And when wilt thou return? So it pleased the king to send me; and I set him a time. Moreover I said unto the king, If it please the king, let letters be given me to the governors beyond the river, that they may convey me over till I come into Judah; And a letter unto Asaph the keeper of the king's forest, that he may give me timber to make beams for the gates of the palace which appertained to the house, and for the wall of the city and for the house that I shall enter into. And the king granted me, according the good hand of my God upon me.

From the time of the beginning of the rebuilding of the temple to the time Christ was crucified was a total of sixty nine years. This left a period of one week or seven years to complete the seventy weeks that Daniel predicted.

The last week of Daniel's prophecy begins when the Antichrist makes a peace agreement with Israel.

Some have made it sound confusing as to how the seventy weeks of Daniel came about. It really isn't that complicated. Daniel prophesied that from the time that the rebuilding of the temple in Jerusalem to the time Christ was crucified would be sixty nine weeks. When the Antichrist makes a peace treaty with Israel would week seventy.

DANIEL 9:27 And he shall confirm the covenant with many for one week.

THE OPENING OF THE SEALS

In chapter six, John begins to use symbols to describe what he saw. Most of the time in the book of Revelation, when symbols are used it is then explained as to what each one means. John starts by telling what he saw as Jesus opens each of the seals. The things that happen when the seals are opened is brought on by the actions of man. The wrath of God will begin at the middle of the great tribulation.

The first four seals that are opened tell about riders on four horses that will have affect on the whole world. The first horse is white, the second is red, the third is black and the fourth is pale. The four horsemen are symbolic but the devastating events on the earth spoken of as the seals are opened are literally true and real. The actions that these four horsemen will have on the world will be awesome.

Mankind has never witnessed the horrible things that will happen during this time. When these seals are opened, there is a possibility that they will overlap one another, meaning that before one action of a seal is finished that the next one is already taking place also.

This will probably happen during the first three and one half years of the tribulation

THE FIRST SEAL

REVELATION 6:1-2 And I saw when the Lamb opened one of the seals, and I heard, as it were the noise of thunder, one of the four beasts saying, come and see. And I saw, and behold a white horse and he that sat on him had a bow; and a crown was given unto him: and he went forth conquering, and to conquer.

I believe that the first half of the great tribulation will start when the rider on the white horse makes peace with Israel.

There are some who believe that the rider on the white horse is Jesus. First of all the white horse is symbolic of the actions of the Antichrist. In the book of Revelation when Jesus comes from heaven riding on a white horse it will be on a literal real horse.

The rider on the white horse has a bow in his hand, but it does not mention arrows. I believe that when he conquers the nations of the world, he will have such power from the nations backing him that the other nations will not even try to defend themselves and will join up with the antichrist rather than fight. This way he gets the nations to join with him through his cunning words and promises. To some he will be the Messiah that they have been waiting for.

When a crown is given him, it is speaking of a crown of authority given by the nations that he leads and will give him all power to do the things he wants to.

After gaining control of the nations on the earth, he will soon see that things are really becoming difficult to handle as other seals are opened by the Lamb of God.

THE SECOND SEAL

REVELATION 6:3-4 And when he had opened the second seal, I heard the second beast say, come and see. And there went out another horse that was red: and power was given to him that sat thereon to take peace from the earth, and that they would kill one another: and there was given unto him a great sword.

Some people believe that the red horse would indicate that the country of Russia would be involved in the conflicts that would take place during this time. No one really knows, but this is possible. After the war of Magog and Israel is over, Russia and their allies would have to regroup and reorganize to be an active force at that time.

The Antichrist will not have complete control at this time of all the nations and will have to literally battle some of them to take control.

The way the verse explains the red horse saying that they would kill one another, there will possibly be a civil war within several countries where they will fight their own countrymen. There will be a lot of bloodshed during this time. During and after a war, there is always destruction of property, homes and food supplies. This will be a time chaos and will usher in the opening of the third seal that brings about the collapse of world economy.

THE THIRD SEAL

REVELATION 6:5-6 And when he had opened the third seal, I heard the third beast say, Come and see. And I beheld, and lo a black horse; and he that sat on him had a pair of balances in his hand. And I heard a voice in the midst of the four beasts say, A measure of wheat for a penny, and three measures of barley for a penny; and see thou hurt not the oil and the wine.

This scripture indicates that there is coming a time on earth when food production will drop to an all time low. Through wars and climate conditions food will be so scarce that what there is available will be so high that a person will have to work all day just to buy a loaf of bread. At the present time it is estimated that over eighteen thousand people starve to death each day around the world and we now produce more food than at any time in history and people are still starving.

It is hard to really visualize a time when food around the world will be produced not by using tractors and other motorized machines, but by ways that food was grown over two hundred years ago using mules and other animals to make a crop.

This will be a time when the fourth seal will come into being when sickness and death will take the lives of so many people around the world.

THE FOURTH SEAL

REVELATION 6:7-8 And when he had opened the fourth seal, I heard the voice of the fourth beast say, Come and see. And I looked, and behold a pale horse: and his name that sat on him was Death, and Hell followed with him. And power was given unto them over the fourth part of the earth, to kill with sword, and with hunger, and with death, and with the beasts of the earth.

This seal will usher in the most devastating blow to living on this earth that has ever come to pass. Wars will be going on all over the world and when wars happen disease and plagues usually take their toll. Without proper medicine and food millions and millions will die.

The scripture tells us that death and hell follow the rider on the pale horse. This could mean that one fourth of the world's population would die from these events. At present there are around six billion people living on earth. This would mean that over one and one half billion people would lose their lives over the world or it could be on a particular continent that has billions of people living on it. Whatever the case this is still a number of deaths that we cannot even imagine in our mind such horror.

There is a part of the scripture about the pale horse that is difficult to understand. This is the part that the beasts of the earth has in this horrific time. Some believe that animals ranging from pets to dangerous ones that live in the forest will suddenly turn on mankind and attack and kill for food or just be driven by satanic possession to kill at will. If all the millions of pets owned by the people of the United States would be start attacking humans this would account for many, many deaths.

THE FIFTH SEAL

REVELATION 6:9-11 And when he had opened the fifth seal, I saw under the altar the souls of them that were slain for the word of God, and for the testimony which they held: And they cried with a loud voice, saying, How long, O Lord, holy and true, dost thou not judge and avenge our blood on them that dwell on the earth? And white robes were given unto every one of them; and it was said unto them, that they should rest yet for a little season, until their fellow servants also and their brethren, that should be killed as they were, should be fulfilled.

The apostle John saw a multitude of souls under the alter of God. These were Christians that had been killed during the first part of the great tribulation. They could either see what was going on at that time on the earth or as the souls of them that were killed entered into heaven told them what was happening on the earth at that time. This answers the question" When we die, will we know what is taking place on earth?" The answer has to be "yes". They were asking God how long before justice would brought upon evil men who were doing the killing on earth.

God understands their anxiety about their fellow men and gives them white robes to wear and assures them that justice would brought about, but there was a certain number of Christians on earth that would die by the sword and then vengeance would take place by his mighty hand.

Sometimes we become anxious when we think that something should be done and we think God should act right away. We should always remember that God has a plan and it is always on time. It is always a perfect plan and when it comes to pass we can then understand why it happened and when it happened was always the right way.

THE SIXTH SEAL

REVELATION 6:12-17 And I beheld when he had opened the

sixth seal, and lo, there was a great earthquake, and the sun became black as sackcloth of hair, and the moon became as blood; And the stars of heaven fell unto the earth, even as a fig tree casteth her untimely figs, when she is shaken of a mighty wind. And the heaven departed as a scroll when it is rolled together; and every mountain and island were moved out of their places. And the kings of the earth, and the great men, and the rich men, and the chief captains, and the mighty men, and every bondman, and every free man hid themselves in the dens and in the rocks of the mountains; And said to the mountains and rocks, fall on us, and hide us from the face of him that sitteth on the throne, and from the wrath of the Lamb; For the great day of his wrath is come; and who shall be able to stand?

Up until this time, catastrophes, death, diseases, starvation, wars, and other bad things that were happening to people around the world were caused by man or the works of Satan. It would appear that when the sixth seal is opened that this is the beginning of the wrath of God that is being poured out upon the earth.

When a great earthquake takes place and the sun is darkened, and the moon seems to turn to blood man will start to believe what Christians were talking about when they tried to warn the people about things that were going to come to pass in the last days. When stars begin to fall to earth and mountains are moved out of their places, unbelievers will cry out to the mountains to fall on them and hid them from God. The stars are probably meteorites that will be falling all over the earth and earthquakes causing smoke and dust to hid the sun and make the moon look as it were blood.

Mankind all over the world will be calling to the mountains to hide them instead of calling upon God to save their souls. The Bible tells us that there will be strong delusions that will be taking place at that time and they will believe that God exists, but will not call on him to save them. The Bible also tells us that even the demons believe that God exists, so just believing God is real is not enough. A person must believe, confess and receive God in their heart in order to be saved.

THE 144,000 JEWS

At some period of time during the opening of the seals, there will a great number of people who will turn to Christ. Some will remember hearing the gospel preached before the rapture, others will find Bibles, tapes and books that believers left behind and come to Christ by reading and listening to them.

During this time there will be a great revival in Israel among the Jews. They will begin to believe in Jesus and a great time of witnessing will take place. The Bible tells us that there will be 144,000 Jews from the twelve tribes of Israel who will be saved and start to witness for Jesus.

REVELATION 7:2-4 And I saw another angel ascending from the east, having the seal of the of the living God; and he cried with a loud voice to the four angels, to whom it was given to hurt the earth and the sea, Saying, hurt not the earth, neither the sea, nor the trees, till we have sealed the servants of our god in their foreheads. And I heard the number of them which were sealed; and there were sealed an hundred and forty and four thousand of all the tribes of the children of Israel.

There will be twelve thousand Jews chosen from each of the twelve tribes of Israel. These Jews could be living all over the world and be saved and start to witness for Christ. Some believe that these Jews will be living in Israel at this time. It really doesn't matter where they are living at this time for God has his hand on them and has a seal put on their forehead so that none of the wrath of God will harm them or any of the evil creatures that come out of the earth will be able to harm them.

They will go forth all over the earth giving the plan of salvation to millions of people and a great revival will take place at this time.

REVELATION 7:1-4 And after these things I saw four angels standing on the four corners of the earth, holding the four winds of the earth, that the wind should not blow on the earth, nor on the sea, nor on any tree. And I saw another angel ascending from the east, having the seal of the living God: and he cried with a loud voice to the four angels, to whom it was given to hurt the earth and the sea, saying, Hurt not the earth, neither the sea nor the trees, till we have sealed the servants of our God in their foreheads. And I heard the number of them which were sealed: and there were sealed an hundred and forty and four thousand of all the tribes of the children of Israel.

REVELATION 14:4-5 These are they which were not defiled with women; for they are virgins. These are they which goeth. These were redeemed from among men, being the first fruits unto God and to the Lamb. And in their mouth was found no guile: for they are without fault before the throne of God.

THE SEVENTH SEAL

REVELATION 8:1-5 And when he had opened the seventh seal, there was silence in heaven about the space of half an hour. And I saw the seven angels which stood before God; and to them were given seven trumpets. And another angel came and stood at the alter, having a golden censer and there was given unto him much incense, that he should offer it with the prayers of all saints upon the golden altar which was before the throne. And the smoke of the incense, which came with the prayers of the saints, ascended up before God out the angel's hand. And the angel took the censer, and filled it with fire of the alter, and cast it into the earth: and there were voices, and thundering, and lightning and an earthquake.

No one can really say for certain why there is silence in heaven for a period of half and hour. Some believe that this is a time when all heaven is silent just before the most devastating time in all history of the earth. This will begin the phases of the wrath of God being brought upon the earth. These actions will come directly from God upon the unsaved inhabitants on earth who have given their allegiance to the forces of evil and have literally shaken their fists in the face of God and said that they want no part of Him.

During this time period, the Antichrist and his followers will have control of most all of the nations and will be ruling them in a Godless society.

Up until now all the havoc that has happened on earth has been made by man or nature with all the pestilences, diseases, starvation and earthquakes. The time has come now for God to pour out his wrath on the earth which the apostle John has recorded in Revelations. This will be going on through the trumpet and bowl judgments right through the time that Satan is thrown out of heaven and links up with the Antichrist and the False Prophet at the middle of the great tribulation.

So now the time has come for the seven angels to sound and the wrath of God is poured out on the earth.

REVELATION 8:6 And the seven angels which had the seven trumpets pre-pared themselves to sound.

THE FIRST TRUMPET

REVELATION 8:7 The first angel sounded, and there followed hail and fire mingled with blood, and they were cast upon the earth: and the third part of trees was burnt up, and all green grass was burnt up.

This is very similar to what happened to Sodom and Gomorrah in the Old Testament only this will be worldwide. One can hardly imagine one of every three trees would be burned and not any green grass left. This would be like an artist drawing a lovely field of grass in a painting and decides to erase all the grass in the picture leaving only bare land.

REVELATION 8:8 And the second angel sounded, and as it were a great mountain burning with fire was cast into the sea: and the third part of the sea became blood.

Some believe that this great mountain burning with fire is a meteorite that will hit the earth somewhere and have such and impact that the very earth under the sea will turn blood red in color. This impact would be for many thousands of miles in diameter and many miles beneath the ocean. This would be similar to what some believe that happened when the dinosaurs became extinct. Tidal waves would be bigger than any tsunami that we can remember.

THE THIRD TRUMPET

REVELATION 8:10-11 And the third angel sounded, and there fell a great star from heaven, burning as it were a lamp, and it fell upon the third part of the rivers, and upon the fountains of waters, and the name of the star is called Wormwood: and the third part of the waters became wormwood; and many men died of the water, because they were made bitter.

This trumpet judgment will be a huge blow to the population of the earth. One third of the rivers will be literally poisoned by this star called "Wormwood", which means poison or a bitter herb in the Bible. Even drinking water will be poisoned and many people will die. Just imagine one third of the population of the earth will be without pure water to survive. This will be a time when people who have excess to clean water will realize that they have taken for granted the pleasure of having pure water to drink daily, but no longer have.

THE FOURTH TRUMPET

REVELATION 8:12-13 And the fourth angel sounded, and the third part of the sun was smitten, and the third part of the moon, and third part of the stars; so as the third part of them was darkened, and the day shone not for a third part of it, and the night likewise. And I beheld, and heard an angel flying through the midst of heaven, saying with a loud voice, Woe, woe, woe, to the inhibitors of the earth by reason of the other voices of the trumpet of the three angels, which are yet to sound!

When the fourth trumpet sounds the whole world will become darkened. The sun, moon and stars will be darkened by one third. This would appear just as the natural light dims when a huge storm approaches. Everyone will become depressed and will just want to get out of all these bad things that are happening, but there is no escape. Even the days and nights will be darkened overall. Some have said that all these effects will be caused from the use of nuclear weapons, but I believe that as God had the power in the beginning to speak light into existence, he will do the same by just turning the lights down through his mighty power just as we would do with a dimmer switch to turn down the light on a light bulb.

The previous trumpet judgments have been bad, but an angel cries with a loud voice saying "Woe, woe, woe to the inhabiters of the earth". He is telling everyone that the first trumpets were only a warm up compared to what is going to happen next.

THE FIFTH TRUMPET

REVELATION 9:1-2 And the fifth angel sounded, and I saw a star fall from heaven unto earth: and to him was given the key of the bottomless pit. And he opened the bottomless pit; and there arose a smoke out of the pit, as the smoke of a great furnace: and the sun and the air were darkened by reason of the smoke of the pit.

John sees a star fall from heaven into the earth and he was given the key to the bottomless pit or Abyss. The star is referred to as a he so this would be an angel with authority to open the bottomless pit. As he opened the pit huge amounts of smoke, so big that the sun was even darkened by it.

Some times in the Bible when the word pit is used it refers to a place of imprisonment of evil spirits.

2 PETER 2:4 For if God spared not the angels that sinned, but cast them down to hell, and delivered them into chains of darkness, to be reserved unto judgment.

JUDE 6 And the angels which kept not their first estate, but left their own habitation, he hath reserved in everlasting chains under darkness unto the judgment of the great day.

REVELATION 9:3-5 And there came out of the smoke locusts upon the earth: and unto them was given power, as the scorpions of the earth have power. And it was commanded them that they should not hurt the grass of the earth, neither any green thing, neither any tree; but only those men which have not the seal of God in their foreheads. And to them it was given that they should not kill them, but that they should be tormented five months:

and their torment was as the torment of a scorpion, when he striketh a man.

Out of the smoke coming out of the pit were swarms of locusts that were ready to devour anything in their path. Locusts are known for their fierce appetite when invading fields of grain and corn. When they go through a field hardly anything is left standing.

These locusts are different. They are super locusts. They have the power of scorpions and are ready to attack, but they are told that they could not hurt the grass and trees or anyone who has the seal of God upon them. This should tell anyone that no matter what is going on that God is still in control of everything.

For five long months the locusts will torture anyone who does not have the seal of God on their foreheads. Life will become so unbearable that they will try to kill themselves, but cannot do it.

REVELATION 9:7-12 And the shapes of the locusts were like unto horses prepared unto battle and on their heads were as it were crowns like gold and their faces were as the faces of men. And they had hair as the hair of women and their teeth were as the teeth of lions. And they had breastplates, as it were breastplates of iron; and the sound of their wings was as the sound of chariots of many horses running to battle. And they had tails like unto scorpions, and there were stings in their tails: and their power was to hurt men five months.

And they had a king over them, which is the angel of the bottomless pit, whose name in the Hebrew tongue is Abaddon, but in the Greek tongue hath his name Apollyon. This is not Satan as some people believe, because he has not been imprisoned for all these years. This being could be a kind of captain of Satan's and will lead this army of locusts to torcher and sting unbelievers.

John had never seen any kind of creatures like this before and all he could do was to describe them as best he could. He did not describe the size of them only that they had a powerful sting in their tails that made men want to kill themselves but could not. This would be a similar situation as was seen in the Alfred Hitchcock movie "The birds". This movie was about a swarm of birds that attached people in a town. They would attack and kill by biting the people with their beaks. These locusts will have unbelievers running and trying to hide from the terrible stings. This will continue for a period of five months during the beginning of the tribulation. Why a period of this time is not explained. This passage of scripture is similar to the time John spoke about in Revelation 6:15-16 when the sixth seal was opened and men wanted the mountains to fall on them because of the earthquakes and mountains being moved out of their places.

THE SIXTH TRUMPET

REVELATION 9:13-15 And the sixth angel sounded, and I heard a voice from the four horns of the golden altar which is before God. Saying to the sixth angel which had the trumpet, loose the four angels which are bound in the great river Euphrates. And the four angels were loosed, which were prepared for an hour, and a day, and a month, and a year, for to slay the third part of men.

The angels that are bound in the Euphrates river are evil angels that were followers of Satan and had done such horrible things at some point in time that God had them bound in the river Euphrates. Knowing that these angels were evil and would attack and kill anyone in their path, God uses them to complete another phase of his wrath upon the unbelieving humans during this time in which a third of mankind will be killed.

These angels will control a mass army of vicious creatures that no human being has ever seen before. Not even the best horror movie producers could come up with anything that could compare with these awful beings.

REVELATION 9:16-19 And the number of the army of the horsemen were two hundred thousand thousand: and I heard the number of them. And thus I saw the horses in the vision, and them that sat on them, having breastplates of fire, and of jacinth, and brimstone: and the heads of the horses were as the heads of lions; and out of their mouths issued fire and smoke and brimstone. By these three was the third part of men killed, by the fire, and by the smoke, and by the brimstone, which issued out of their mouths. For their power is in their mouth, and in their tails: for their tails were like unto serpents, and had heads, and with them they do hurt.

These creatures were riding something that to John looked similar to a horse with a head like a lion and spewing fire, smoke and brimstone out of their mouths.

John could not possible count all these creatures, so God gave him a figure of two hundred million.

A lot of writers and prophecy teachers have taken this verse out of context and have claimed that these are a literal army of human beings probably from China riding on horses and are attacking Israel. Why would an army of that size attack a country of only five or six million people? An army of that size riding horses would be over ten miles deep and nearly one hundred miles wide. This would make no sense at all. The scripture clearly states that these creatures come from out of the Euphrates river and will attack the entire world until one third of the population is killed. One can hardly imagine the slaughter of two billion people. It would be like the whole country of China being destroyed, which has an estimated population of one billion and three hundred million inhabitants at present.

All of the one third of mankind that is destroyed would be unbelievers. The question is asked "why just unbelievers?" Simply because, in past history, God never sends his wrath upon his children. Christians will suffer by the hand of man, but not from the wrath of God.

REVELATION 9:20-21 And the rest of the men which were not killed by these plagues yet repented not of the works of their hands, that they should not worship devils, and idols of gold, and silver and brass, and stone, and of wood; which neither can see, nor hear, nor walk: Neither repented they of their murders, nor of their sorceries, nor of their fornication, nor of their thefts.

Even after seeing millions upon millions of people killed before their very eyes, the remaining men would not give up their carnal nature of worshipping devils, and idols made of metal and stone. They continued in their immoral way of life of murdering, robbing and fornication. We are told that in the end times that God would send strong delusion and that would believe a lie.

2 THESSALONIANS 2:11-12 And for this cause God shall send them strong delusion, that they should believe a lie; That they all might be damned who believed not the truth, but had pleasure in unrighteousness.

THE SEVENTH TRUMPET

And the seventh angel sounded, and there were great voices in heaven, saying "The kingdoms of this world are become the kingdoms of our Lord, and of his Christ; and he shall reign forever and ever. And the temple of God was opened in heaven, and there was seen in his temple the ark of his testament; and there were lightning, and voices, and thundering, and an earthquake, and great hail.

When the seventh angel sounds, all of heaven will declare the majesty of the God of heaven. All creatures will worship God and tell him what great things he has done.

The apostle John looks inside the temple and sees the ark of his testament. There are many thoughts about this verse. Some say that the Ark of the Covenant that has been lost for centuries had been transported to heaven. Others believe this ark was always in heaven and that the ark that God told Moses how to build was just a model of the real one in heaven. Some who believe this thought hope that when the new temple is built in Jerusalem, the original ark that Moses had built will show up and be placed in the temple.

From most Christian's view, it doesn't really matter, because God has a plan and it is always right.

CHAPTER SEVEN

MID-TRIBULATION

At this point in time, after the seven seals have been opened and the angels with the seven trumpets have sounded, the Antichrist, Satan and the False Prophet will come on the scene with destruction and chaos to all the world for the next three and one half years.

The Antichrist had made a peace treaty with Israel and other countries of the world, but things start to happen in the spiritual realm that will upset all things for the next three and one half years. Satan will be tossed out of the heavens down to the earth.

REVELATION 12:7-12 And there was war in heaven: Michael and his angels fought against the dragon; and the dragon fought and his angels, and prevailed not; neither was their place found any more in heaven. And the great dragon was cast out, that old serpent, called the Devil, and Satan, which deceiveth the whole world; he was cast out into the earth, and his angels were cast out with him. And I heard a loud voice saying in heaven, Now is come salvation and strength, and the kingdom of our God, and the power of his Christ; for the accuser of our brethren is cast down, which accused them before our God day and night. And they overcame him by the blood o9f the Lamb, and by the word of their testimony, and they loved not their lives unto the death. Therefore rejoice, ye heavens, and ye that dwell in them. Woe to the inhabiters of the earth and of the sea! For the devil is come down unto you, having great wrath, because he knoweth that he hath but a short time.

There was a great war in heaven consisting of millions of good angels and the evil angels who had followed Satan when he tried to ascend to the throne of heaven and be as God. God had allowed Satan to have access to the third heaven where he abodes, and he would come to the throne and accuse the believers living on the earth of wrong doings that they had committed.

While the great tribulation is taking place on earth, something happened in heaven and causes Satan and Michael the archangel with their angels to have a war. After the battle is over, Michael and his angels defeat Satan so he was cast down to the earth for he could no longer stay in the area of heaven.

Satan has always taken advantage of every situation in order to gain anything for himself and when he sees the activities of the Antichrist and the things that he is doing on earth, he sees a way that he can continue to destroy and kill on the earth. He finds a way that he can literally possess the body of the Antichrist and do his evil deeds.

REVELATION 13:3-7 And I saw one of his heads as it were wounded to death; and his deadly wound was healed: and all the world wondered after the beast. And they worshipped the dragon which gave power unto the beast: and they worshipped the beast, saying, Who is like unto the beast? Who is able to make war with him? And there was given unto him a mouth speaking great things and blasphemies; and power was given unto him to continue forty and two months. And he opened his mouth in blasphemy against God, to blaspheme his name, and his tabernacle, and them that dwell in heaven. And it was given unto him to make war with the saints, and to overcome them; and power was given him over all kindreds, and tongues, and nations, and all that well upon the earth shall worship him, whose names are not written in the book of life of the Lamb slain from the foundation of the world.

The Antichrist suffers a deadly wound to his head and actually dies. The scripture does not say who is responsible for dealing the

Antichrist this deadly wound, but is probably someone who he had harmed and was wanting to get revenge.

This is when Satan comes on the scene and actually uses his spiritual power to raise him up and brings him to life again. Some would say "only God can bring someone back from the dead." No one needs to be fooled into thinking that Satan does not have a lot of power, for the scripture says that he goes about seeking whom he may devour. God permits him to raise the Antichrist up for a specific purpose during this period of time.

Satan then possesses the Antichrist's soul and body and starts to do the evil work that he has planned. When the Antichrist is raised up he immediately starts to change the things of the past three and one half years and destroy the functions of the Jews in Jerusalem and stop the daily sacrifices in the temple.

REVELATION 24:15-16 When ye therefore shall see the abomination of desolation, spoken of by Daniel the prophet, stand in the holy place (whoso readeth, let him understand). Then let them which be in Judea flee into the mountains.

DANIEL 9: 27 And he shall confirm the covenant with many for one week; and in the midst of the week he shall cause the sacrifice and the oblation to cease, and for the overspreading of abominations he shall make it desolate, even until the consummation, and that determined shall be poured upon the desolate.

DANIEL 12:11 And from the time that the daily sacrifice shall be taken away, and the abomination that maketh desolate set up, there shall be a thousand two hundred and ninety days.

Then Satan speaks through the Antichrist as he stands in the temple and announces that there will no longer be any sacrifices and burnt offerings given in the temple.

The next few verses tell about a women clothed with the sun is about to give birth to a child.

REVELATION 12:1-2, 5, 13 And there appeared a great

Chapter Seven: Mid-Tribulation | 89

wonder in heaven; a woman clothed with the sun, and the moon under her feet, and upon her head a crown of twelve stars: and she being with child cried, travailing in birth, and pained to be delivered. 5- And she brought forth a man child, who was to rule all nations with a rod of iron: and her child was caught up unto God, and to his throne. 6- And the woman fled into the wilderness, where she hath a place prepared of God, that they should feed her there a thousand two hundred and threescore days.

Just about everyone agrees that the woman in these verses is the nation of Israel. The most logical answer as to who the child is would be Jesus. The question that comes to mind in a lot of people is the fact that when John wrote the book of Revelation, the first three chapters pertained to the present time that he was living in. The remainder of the chapters told about the events that would take place in the future. If the woman was Israel and the child being Jesus, why would a history of the past be included among the future events? Some have asked if this was Jesus, why would Israel flee to the mountains after he was caught up to be with God?

Some teachers believe that the child is the 144,000 witnesses, because they appear to be in heaven in chapter 14. They believe that their mission is done when the Antichrist tries to hunt them down and kill them.

REVELATION 14:1 And I looked, and, lo, a Lamb stood on the mount Zion, and with him an hundred forty and four thousand, having his Father's name written in their foreheads.

Some believe that these witnesses were caught up to God after their mission of witnessing was done.

REVELATION 14:2-4 And I heard a voice from heaven, as the voice of many waters, and as the voice of a great thunder, and I heard the voice of harpers harping with their harps. And they sung as it were a new song before the throne, and before the four beasts, and the elders, and no man could learn that song but the hundred and forty and four thousand, which were redeemed from the earth. These are they which were not defiled with women; for they are virgins. These are they which follow the Lamb whithersoever he goeth. These were redeemed from among men, being the first fruits unto God and to the Lamb.

Everyone has their own thoughts and opinions as to who the scripture is talking about and it really doesn't matter who is right, because God knows and that is what counts.

After the birth of the child, the woman who is Israel flees to a place of refuge to stay unharmed for a period of three and one half years or until the battle of Armageddon is over.

After the persecution and killing of the Jews in Jerusalem the number left would be down considerable. There are around six million Jews in Israel today. Some have said that there would be about one million left to seek safety when the Antichrist tries to slaughter all of them.

There is a place in Jordan called Petra, which is a place in the mountains where long ago a civilization lived and living quarters are hewn out in the rocks. The passage way that leads into the city is very narrow that even a car could not get through and is the perfect place of protection. It is about sixty miles from Jerusalem and could provide a living place for about one million people. A lot of people believe that this is the place that the Jews will go when the Antichrist pursues them.

This is another situation where I believe that the world will be as it were over two hundred years ago without electricity or modern day weapons of war. If there were modern weapons of war with planes and tanks, why wouldn't the Antichrist just bomb the city of Petra and kill all the Jews? This would be as easy as it was when the Japanese bombed Pearl Harbor in 1941.

THE TWO WITNESSES

Some people believe that two witnesses will appear in Jerusalem at the beginning of the tribulation period, while others believe that they will appear at the middle of this period. I believe that they will come on the scene at the middle of the great tribulation and will witness to the Jews in Israel for three and one half years. This will be the time when the Antichrist and the False Prophet will be in full power and he will claim that he is god. Chapter eleven tells to whole story of the actions of the two witnesses and what they will be doing for the years they live on earth.

REVELATION 11:3-6 And I will give power unto my two witnesses, and they shall prophesy a thousand two hundred and threescore days, clothed in sackcloth. These are the two olive trees and the two candlesticks standing before the God of the earth. And if any man will hurt them, fire proceddeth out of their mouth and devoured their enemies; and if any man will hurt them, he must in this manner be killed. These have power to shut heaven, that it rain not in the days of their prophecy; and have power over waters to turn them to blood, and to smite the earth with all plagues, as often as they will.

ZECHARIAH 4:1-3 And the angel that talked with me came again, and waked me, as a man that is wakened out of his sleep And said unto me, What seest thou? And I said I have looked and behold a candlestick all of gold, with a bowl upon the top of it, and his seven lamps thereon, and seven pipes to the seven lamps, which are upon the top thereof: And two olive trees by it, one upon the right side of the bowl, and the other upon the left side thereof.

The apostle John and Zechariah looked into the throne room of God and saw two olive trees standing by the lamp stands, which is really the two witnesses who will descend upon the earth for a period of three and one half years.

There has been much speculation as to who these two men are. They will have to be someone who is in heaven already so they cannot be anyone who would be living on the earth at that time.

Some think that one of them is Moses because he appeared with Elijah on the mount of transfiguration and that he brought many miracles and plagues upon the Egyptians during the time the Israelites were in bondage.

Others say that one of them is Elijah, because he never died a physical death, but was taken up by a whirlwind into heaven.

Enoch is another possibility. It is recorded in the book of Genesis that he walked with God and he was not for God took him.

Regardless who the witnesses are, God knows and has them on a special assignment to be a witness for him in the land of Israel. No information is given as to how they show up to start their work at this time, but they are anointed and powerful. They will have the power to defend themselves by fire coming from their mouths and destroying their enemies. They will be a thorn in the flesh to the Antichrist. During the three and a half years he will do everything in his power to kill them, but they are protected by God until it is their time to ascend to heaven.

They will have the power to shut up the heavens and no rain will fall for the time that they are on the earth. They will be able to bring about plagues whenever they see fit. They will be continually harassed by the Antichrist and the unbelievers day and night and when they come to the point that something has to be done they will use their God given power and bring about what ever punishment is necessary to combat the enemy.

They will win thousands of souls to Jesus through their witnessing. This is what will cause the Antichrist to hate them so much, but there is nothing he can do about it until God is ready to take them home.

REVELATION 11:7-13 And when they shall have finished their testimony, the beast that ascendeth out of the bottomless pit shall make war against them, and shall overcome them, and kill them. And their dead bodies shall lie in the street of the great city, which spiritually is called Sodom and Egypt, where also our Lord was crucified. And they of the people and kindreds and tongues and nations shall see their dead bodies three days and an half, and shall not suffer their dead bodies to be put in graves. And they that dwell upon the earth shall rejoice over them, and make merry, and shall send gifts one to another, because these two prophets tormented them that dwelt on the earth. And after three days and an half the Spirit of life from God entered into them, and they stood upon their feet, and great fear fell upon them which saw them. And they heard a great voice from heaven saying unto them, come up hither. And they ascended up to heaven in a cloud, and their enemies beheld them. And the same hour was there a great earthquake, and the tenth part of the city fell, and in the earthquake were slain of men seven thousand and the remnant were affrighted, and gave glory to the God of heaven.

After three and one half years it is time for them to be taken home to heaven and he allows the Antichrist to make war with them and kill them. Their dead bodies will lie in the the streets of Jerusalem. The unbelievers who have been tormented by the witnesses will be jubilant and happy that they have been killed and will send presents to one another in celebration for this event. They will not even allow their bodies to be buried, but leave them in the streets to start to decay.

People from all over the world will get to see their bodies and rejoice. For a long time this statement has brought about how it would be possible for the world to see them. The answer came when TV was invented so now it is possible for everyone to see through the efforts of the news media.

What will be so amazing about this event is the fact that after three and one half days these two witnesses will slowly rise to their feet and fear will fall upon the people observing them. Then they heard a voice from heaven saying "come up hither." Then they ascended up to heaven in a cloud. Their enemies were astounded and could not believe what was happening.

They will be witnessing an event that had not happened in over two thousand years and that was when Jesus ascended from the Mount of Olives into heaven.

At the same time that this event happened there was a great earthquake in the city and seven thousand were killed. And the scripture says that those that were left glorified God and I believe were saved that day.

Some time before and during the tribulation period, the whole world will have experienced a period of time when there is a new world order with the antichrist as president and leader and a worldwide religion that will probably be led by the false prophet. Everyone will be expected to obey both of these leaders or face serious problems even their lives taken.

The False Prophet will be given tremendous power by Satan to carry out the work of the Antichrist.

REVELATION 13:16-18 And he causeth all, both small and great, rich and poor, free and bond, to receive a mark in their right hand, or on their foreheads: And that no man might buy or sell save he that had the mark, or the name of the beast, or the number of his name. Here is wisdom. Let him that hath understanding count the number of the beast: for it is the number of a man; and his number is Six hundred threescore and six.

There have been many books and articles written about the mark of the beast. Some writers claiming that they know who the name of the Antichrist is by using some kind of formula of names and numbers. Some people have become paranoid about the numbers 666. When the number 666 appears on drivers licenses, social security cards, auto tags and various identification numbers, some people become almost frantic and want to have them changed.

The mark of the beast will placed on the forehead or on the right hand. In these days of modern technology, marks of different types could be used. Marks on the skin that could only be seen under a certain type light or implants under the skin that could carry a person's own medical history or other personal information about them.

In our present day, a lot is being said about creating a one world order in which everyone would have to have their medical and personal history stored through an implant in their body so the government could have access to it at any time. It is almost like that now, with the communications the way it is and so many people having access to personal computers with e mail and face book. Some sources say even now that anyone who has ever used the internet has vital information about them stored in master computers in some parts of the world.

In the last fifty years the number 666 has became very popular after being used in movies, books and articles where the number is always used in connection with some kind of fear of being harmed or killed.

The real truth is that most that fear these numbers are not familiar with the Bible enough to know that this will only occur during the tribulation period and that Christians living today will be raptured before this takes place.

This will be a horrible time. Individuals and families will have to make a choice between taking the mark of the beast and living and being able to buy food to survive or not taking the mark and risk being killed or starve to death.

The bible tells us that after a person takes the mark of the beast that there will no longer be a chance of redemption for them.

REVELATION 14:11 And the smoke of their torment ascendeth up forever and ever: and they have no rest day nor night, who worship the beast and his image, and whosoever receiveth the mark of his name.

Some Bible teachers believe that the mark of the beast will only be used in Israel rather than all nations on earth. They take in consideration that there will still be some nations that are under the rule of the one world order, but have their own rules of their country to abide by.

At this time Satan has taken complete control of the Antichrist and is controlling all actions of the people. In Jerusalem he is acting like a god on a throne. He remembers how Jesus rose from the dead and wants to connect the rising of the Antichrist in the same way. He wants so much to be like God in every way and deep down inside he truly that in some way this will come to pass.

A lot of things have come to pass since the Antichrist came on the scene and began to lead the world. The following is just a few of the things that has transpired.

* A one world government has been established.
* Rome has become the capital of the Antichrist.
* In Rome, a world religion led by the False Prophet has been established.
* The seven seals have been broken.
* The four horsemen have led the entire world into chaos.
* The seven trumpets of God have sounded.
* One third of the nations vegetation have been destroyed.
* One third of the sea has turned to blood.
* One third of the rivers have turned to blood.
* Great earthquakes have shaken the world.
* One third of mankind has been killed.
* Plaques of demonic locusts have attacked man.
* Satan and his angels have been thrown from heaven down to earth.
* The Antichrist has been slain and then revived by Satan where he has possessed his body.
* Millions of Christians have been killed for not submitting to the demands of the antichrist.

The time has come now for God to order his angels to pour out the vials of wrath.

REVELATION 16:1-2 And I heard a great voice out of the temple saying to the seven angels, Go your ways, and pour out the vials of the wrath of God upon the earth. And the first went, and poured out his vial upon the earth; and there fell a noisome and grievous sore upon the men which had the mark of the beast, and upon them which worshipped his image.

Not only were the people who received the mark of the beast doomed to hell, but they were to suffer all the physical sores upon their bodies. This agonizing pain would make them remember that they once had a choice to reject the mark of the beast but refused to obtain temporal food and protection.

REVELATION 16:3-4 and the second angel poured out his vial upon the sea; and it became as the blood of a dead man: and every living soul died in the sea. And the third angel poured out his vial upon the rivers and fountains of waters, and they became blood.

Everywhere a person looked where clean clear water used to be was blood. This is hard to even imagine, but according to God's Word this is how it is going to be in the end times.

REVELATION 16:8-9 And the fourth angel poured out his vial upon the sun; and power was given unto him to scorch men with fire. And men were scorched with great heat, and blasphemed the name of God, which hath power over these plagues: and they repented not to give him glory.

It is hard to visualize how all this heat from the sun will come down, but it would seem to be like a person standing close to a fire and suddenly flames just seem to leap out and strike causing severe burns. People who were being burned were not pleading to God to stop the pain, but were blaspheming God for his actions.

REVELATION 16:10-11 And the fifth angel poured out his vial upon the seat of the beast; and his kingdom was full of darkness, and they gnawed their tongues for pain, and blasphemed the God of heaven because of their pains and their sores, and repented not of their deeds.

The abode of the beast probably refers to Rome where the Antichrist originally had his headquarters. Darkness seemed to engulf this city and was so depressing that they gnawed their tongues while they endured the pain of their sores and still they blasphemed God.

REVELATION 16:12 And the sixth angel poured out his vial upon the great river Euphrates; and the water thereof was dried up, that the way of the kings of the east might be prepared.

The kings of the east probably mean the nation of China which would be headed for Jerusalem to unite with the rest of the nations of the world to fight at the battle of Armageddon.

Before the seventh angel pours out his great wrath, we will take a glimpse at the world religion and the great city called Babylon.

THE OLD CITY OF BABYLON

The ancient city of Babylon in Iraq is located about 50 south of the city of Bagdad. It was one of the greatest cities of ancient times. Most of the magnificent structures were built by King Nebuchadnezzar around 500 BC. The city was 196 square and was surrounded by walls 14 miles long, 187 feet thick and 200 feet high. Towers extended another 100 feet above the walls. The hanging gardens were one of the wonders of the world.

Today all that is left of Babylon is shambles. No trace of the mighty walls can be found and only a few people occupy the ruins of the once great city. The destruction was prophesied by the prophet Jeremiah.

JEREMIAH 51:58, 62 Thus saith the Lord of host; The broad walls of Babylon shall be utterly broken, and her high gates shall be burned with fire; and the people shall labor in vain, and the folk in the fire, and they shall be weary. (62) Then shalt thou say, O Lord, thou hast spoken against this place, to cut it off, that none shall remain in it, neither man nor beast, but that it shall be desolate forever.

In the book of Revelation in the 18th and 19th chapters, John describes a city called Babylon that will be destroyed by God's wrath when the seventh angel pours out his vial upon it.

THE END TIMES CITY OF BABYLON

Some teachers today say that the old city of Babylon will be rebuilt and prosper in the end times. Others say that this could not be because of the prophecy of Jeremiah that it would never be rebuilt.

Other writers contend that the word Babylon was used when speaking of the city of Rome in the ancient times, therefore when

Babylon is spoken of in the book of Revelation that it is actually referring to Rome. When the apostle Peter ended his 1st epistle to the church in Rome he ended with these words.

1 PETER 5:13 The church that is at Babylon, elected together with you, saluteth you; and so doth Marcus my son.

Another reason to believe that this city is Rome is found in Revelation 18.

REVELATION 18:17-19 For in one hour so great riches is come to naught. And every shipmaster, and all the company in ships, and sailors, and as many as trade by sea, stood afar off. And cried when they saw the smoke of her burning saying, What city is like unto this great city! And they cast dust on their heads, and cried, weeping and wailing, saying, Alas, alas, that great city, wherein were made rich all that had ships in the season of her costliness! for in one hour is she made desolate.

This passage speaks of ships being in the area and trading with the city and watching it be destroyed from the sea. The old city of Babylon has no seaports, but the city of Rome does.

When you think of the the huge city of Bagdad just 50 miles from the old city of Babylon, it would seem odd to rebuild another city that close.

In Revelation chapter 18, an angel cried mightily about the city of Babylon being destroyed and about how evil it had been. It was a place of wickedness where kings and merchants had become drunk of the wrath of her fornication.

REVELATION 18:3 For all nations have drunk of the wine of the wrath of her fornication, and the kings of the earth have committed fornication with her, and the merchants of the earth are waxed rich through the abundance of her delicacies.

The angel mentions several times in this chapter about the city being destroyed in one hour. When the seventh angel pours out his vial, it would appear to be as it was when God destroyed the cities of Sodom and Gomorrah in the Old Testament. Nothing will be left standing as some people will stand a far off looking at the destruction, but would not get close because of harm coming to them.

REVELATION 16:17-21   And the seventh angel poured out his vial into the air; and there came a great voice out of the temple of heaven, from the throne, saying, It is done. And there were voices and thunders, and lightning; and there was a great, such as was not since men were upon the earth, so mighty an earthquake, and so great. And the great city was divided into three parts, and the cities of the nations fell: and great Babylon cam in remembrance before God to give unto her the cup of the wine of the fierceness of his wrath. And every island fled away, and mountains were not found. And there fell upon men a great hail out of heaven, every stone about the weight of a talent: and men blasphemed God because of the plague of the hail; for the plague thereof was exceeding great.

Mankind has never seen such devastation that will take place on earth when God pours out his wrath on this area. Still man will blaspheme God while this is taking place.

This event will usher in the gathering of all nations to fight at the great battle of Armageddon.

In Chapter 17 of Revelation, it also speaks of another Babylon.

MYSTERY BABYLON

REVELATION 17:1-4   And there came one of the seven angels which had the seven vials, and talked with me saying unto me, Come hither; I will show unto thee the judgment of the great whore that sitteth upon many waters: With whom the kings of the earth have committed fornication, and the inhabitants of the earth have been made drunk with the wine of her fornication. So he carried me away in the spirit into the wilderness; and I saw a woman sit upon a scarlet colored beast, full of names of blasphemy, having seven heads and ten horns. And the woman was arrayed in purple and scarlet color, and decked with gold and precious stones and pearls, having a golden cup in her hand full of abominations and filthiness of her fornication. And upon her forehead was a name written, MYSTERY, BABYLON THE GREAT, THE MOTHER OF HARLOTS AND ABOMINATIONS OF THE EARTH.

This MYSTERY BABYLON THE GREAT is a world religion that has its headquarters in this city called Babylon. Most of the world seems to have fallen for a religion that is led by the false prophet. It is a religion that has committed spiritual adultery by completely allowing permissiveness to creep in and will allow immorality to be a common thing. It will be a blend of all religions that will be easy to follow with no obedience to Jesus.

All indications are that it is a world religion, but the fact remains that with over one billion people are Muslims and millions of Hindus and Protestants around the world so it would have to be a type religion that would so liberal in nature that a person would have very few commitments to a God that they professed faith in.

A lot of statements have been made as to what this religion is. Some have indicated that it is the Roman Catholic Church. The reason being that the colors of the church are purple and scarlet as used by the Pope and Cardinals. Also mentioned was the golden cup in her hand indicating that this is a very rich church.

Some believe that this church dates back to the age when thousands of people were put to death in the name of religion during the 14th- 15th centuries.

Some also believe that the False Prophet will be the leader of this world religion with its headquarters in Babylon (or Rome).

REVELATION 17:9 And here is the mind which hath wisdom. The seven heads are seven mountains, on which the woman sitteth.

The city of Rome is known for being located on seven hills. This verse could be more evidence that Rome is really Babylon spoken of in this chapter.

The woman that John speaks about in Rev. 17 is actually a city that the Antichrist reigns from.

REVELATION 17:18 And the woman which thou sawest is that great city, which reigneth over the kings of the earth.

CHAPTER EIGHT

ARMAGEDDON

The word Armageddon has been used over the past few decades in reference to coming events that will eventually take place on earth. Some believe Armageddon will mean the end of the world. Some believe that when nuclear devices are exploded around the world that Armageddon will take place. A few years ago a movie by the name of Armageddon was produced about a meteor that was headed toward earth and when it hit it would be Armageddon.

After World War Two, Gen. Douglas MacArthur made a statement using the word Armageddon. He said " If we do not devise some greater and more equitable means of settling disputes among nations, Armageddon will be at our door."

Most people today are really unfamiliar with the real meaning of the word Armageddon. It is just a handy word to use when talking about a subject that is connected with a mass destruction of something.

The word "Armageddon" comes from a Hebrew word Har-Magedone, which means "Mount Megiddo". It is found only once in the bible in Revelation 16:16, " Then they gathered the kings together to the place that in Hebrew is called Armageddon." There is a place some sixty miles north of Jerusalem that is called the plain of Megiddo that is about sixty miles wide and two hundred miles long. More than two hundred battles have been fought in that region. There is another name that refers to this region and that is the valley of Jehoshaphat. Reference to this is found in Joel 3:2 " I will also gather all nations, and will bring them down into the valley of Jehoshaphat, and will plead with them there for my people and for my heritage Israel, whom they have scattered among the nations, and parted my land."

WHEN WILL THIS BATTLE OCCUR?

The exact time of this battle is a little in the gray area, but several passages in the Bible lead us to believe that it will occur at the end of the seven years of the great tribulation.

In the book of Daniel it tells us that the seventieth year of Daniel's prophecy will start when the Antichrist stands in the temple and confirms a peace treaty with Israel. After three and one half years he breaks the treaty and causes the sacrifice and the oblation to cease in the temple. He then is under the complete power of Satan and declares war upon all believers.

DANIEL 9:27 And he shall confirm the covenant with many for one week: and in the midst of the week he shall cause the sacrifice and the oblation to cease, and for the overspreading of abominations he shall make it desolate, even until the consummation, and that determined shall be poured upon the desolate.

In Daniel also it tells us that after the daily sacrifice is taken away that there will be a thousand two hundred and ninety days.

DANIEL 12:7 And I heard the man clothed in linen, which was upon the waters of the river, when he held up his right hand and his left hand unto heaven, and sware by him that liveth for ever that it shall be for a time, times, and an half; and when he shall have accomplished to scatter the power of the holy people, all these things shall be finished.

DANIEL 12:11 And from the time that the daily sacrifice shall be taken away, and the abomination that maketh desolate set up, there shall be a thousand two hundred and ninety days.

In the book of Matthew it gives additional information about the start of Armageddon.

MATTHEW 24:29-30 Immediately after the tribulation of those days shall the sun be darkened, and the moon shall not give her light, and the stars shall fall from heaven, and the powers of the heavens shall be shaken: And then shall appear the sign of the Son of man in heaven: and then shall all the tribes of the earth mourn, and they shall see the Son of man coming in the clouds of heaven with power and great glory.

After putting these verses together, it would seem to indicate that after the Antichrist has persecuted the believers for three and one half years that the Lord will act and destroy His enemies in the greatest war that man has ever known.

No one but the Lord knows when the rapture will take place, but in the seven years of tribulation when people are being saved, I believe that there will be enough copies of God's word left on earth along with books and other literature that the new Christians can read and see that when the Antichrist stands in the temple and stops the sacrifices that it will only be three and one half years before the battle of Armageddon will take place and Jesus and all the armies of heaven. I also believe that there will be unbelievers that have access to the word of God that will actually be ready at the end of the three and one half years to be prepared to go to battle with Jesus believing in some way that they can defeat Him.

WHAT HAPPENS IN THIS BATTLE?

God says in Joel, "I will also gather all nations, and bring them down to the Valley of Jehoshaphat" (3:2) God will gather all nations to this valley just as He did when He drew Gog and Magog and many nations to fight against Israel as described in the book of Ezekiel. Some believe that the battle of Gog and Magog in Ezekiel is the same battle that is called Armageddon. In Ezekiel the nations that are involved is named. A lot of nations are left out so this could not be the last battle. He says that "He will gather all nations". This means even the United States of America who has been a supporter of Israel ever since it became a nation in 1948 will be with all the other nations. No one knows what will happen to America during this time. It could be that for some reason it sees fit to stop being an ally of Israel, or it could cease to being a supper power and has no choice. Never the less the whole world will come to fight in this valley.

ZECHARIAH 14:2-3 For I will gather all nations against Jerusalem to battle; and the city shall be taken, and the houses rifled, and the women ravished; and half of the city shall go forth into captivity, and the residue of the people shall not be cut off from the city. Then shall the Lord go forth, and fight against those nations, as when he fought in the day of battle.

ZECHARIAH 14:12 And this shall be the plague wherewith the LORD will smite all the people that have fought against Jerusalem; Their flesh shall consume away while they stand upon their feet, and their eyes shall consume away in their holes, and their tongue shall consume away in their mouth.

For a short period of time -- it could be just a day, the enemy of Jerusalem will think that they have won the battle for the city, but it is at this time the Lord will come and annihilate them completely.

A lot of people will say that the situation of flesh falling from the bodies of men and eyes being consumed in their holes indicates that this is a reaction from atomic warfare by mankind. I personally believe that this is the wrath of God being poured out on his enemies at this time. This is the reason there is so much blood in the valley of Megiddo when hundreds of thousands of the enemies of Jerusalem are slaughtered that day.

It seems to be that all the nations want to defeat the nation of Israel and greed has caused all of them to want it for themselves. Another reason is the fact that having heard of Jesus coming back about this time, they will actually think that they might have a chance to defeat Him and all the angels of God. You might say

Chapter Eight: Armageddon | 107

"this is ridiculous, no one can defeat God". No one knows just what ideas and brain-washing that the Antichrist and Satan can do when they get inside the minds of people that they control. They can convince them that they can defeat anyone or anything. This will be similar to the false prophet Jim Jones when he convinced over nine hundred people to follow him to Guyana, South America believing him to be God and all ended up killing themselves by drinking poison.

There are three references to the battle of Armageddon in the book of Revelation. The first is:

REVELATION 19:12-16 And the sixth angel poured out his vial upon the great river Euphrates; and the water thereof was dried up, that the way of the kings of the east might be prepared. And I saw three unclean spirits like frogs come out of the mouth of the dragon, and out of the mouth of the beast, and out of the mouth of the false prophet. For they are the spirits of devils, working miracles, which go forth unto the kings of the earth and of the whole world, to gather them to the battle of that great day of God Almighty. Behold, I come as a thief. Blessed is he that watcheth, and keepeth his garments, lest he walk naked, and they see his shame. And the gathered them together into a place called in the Hebrew tongue Armageddon.

God prepares for this battle when the sixth angel pours out his vial on earth upon the river Euphrates and causes it to dry up. This will allow the kings of the east which is presumed to be China to cross over toward Israel.

This is just one more reason to believe that this battle will be fought with primitive weapons. In modern day warfare there would be planes that could carry numerous troops along with ships and other means of transportation over the river.

John saw unclean spirits coming out of Satan, the Antichrist and the False Prophet that were drawing all nations to this one and final battle. Every nation on the face of the earth could not resist being a part of this battle.

The next mention of this battle is found in an earlier chapter of Revelation. This is one of the reasons that I am led to believe that the book of Revelation is not written in chronological order. I believe that John wrote these passages as the Holy Spirit gave him remembrance after seeing all these things that were to happen in the future. An example of what I am talking about would be like a person spending a day at Six Flags Amusement Park. Most of the time a person will pick up a map of the park that has each place numbered to go by, but hardly anyone goes by the map. Afterward when they are telling someone about what all they saw, hardly anyone will tell the exact sequence that they saw the events they went to. Of the ten events they went to, the second one could actually have been the last one the saw. They are just telling what they remember seeing just not in the exact sequence that it was seen. This is why I believe that the things that happened in Revelation chapter 16 will happen before those in chapter 14.

Never the less in Revelation chapter 14 we read:

REVELATION 14:14-20 And I looked, and behold a white cloud, and upon the cloud one sat like unto the Son of man, having on his head a golden crown, and in his hand a sharp sickle. And another angel came out of the temple, crying with a loud voice to him that sat on the cloud, Thrust in thy sickle, and reap: for the time is come for thee to reap, for the harvest of the earth is ripe. And he that sat on the cloud thrust in his sickle on the earth: and the earth was reaped. And another angel came out of the temple which is in heaven, he also having a sharp sickle. And another angel came out from the altar, which had power over fire, and crying with a loud cry to him that sat on the cloud Thrust in thy sharp sickle, and gather the clusters of the vine of the earth; for her grapes are fully ripe. And the angel thrust in his sickle into the earth, and gathered the vine of the earth, and cast it into the great winepress of the wrath of God. And the winepress was trodden without the city, and blood came out of the winepress, even unto the horse bridles, by the space of a thousand and six hundred furlongs.

Most believe that the one mentioned being on a cloud and

wearing a golden crown is Jesus. Others believe that this could not be Jesus because of the angel coming out of the temple telling him to cast in the sickle and reap. However, this is the time that has come to destroy the armies of all the nations gathered in the valley and the reaping begins. One cannot imagine the outcome of this gruesome battle that takes place. There must be hundreds of thousands that have gathered for battle and it is over in a short time by the hand of Jesus.

The valley of Miggido where they are gathered is said to be about two hundred miles long and about twenty miles wide. After the battle is over, there will be so much blood that has been lost that it will reach as high as a horse's bridle.

The above verse seems to be kind of summary of how the battle will be handled by Jesus. The next verse goes more in detail Jesus coming with his armies.

REVELATION 19:11-21 And I saw heaven opened, and behold a white horse; and he that sat upon him was called Faithful and True, and in righteousness he doth judge and make war. His eyes were as a flame of fire, and on his head were many crowns; and he had a name written, that no man knew, but he himself. And he was clothed with a vesture dipped in blood: and his name is called The Word of God. And the armies which were in heaven followed him upon white horses, clothed in fine linen, white and clean. And out of his mouth goeth a sharp sword, that with it he should smite the nations: and he shall rule them with a rod of iron: and he treadeth the winepress of the fierceness and wrath of Almighty God. And he hath on his vesture and on his thigh a name written, KING OF KINGS, AND LORD OF LORDS.

And I saw an angel standing in the sun; and he cried with a loud voice, saying to all the fowls that fly in the midst of heaven, Come and gather yourselves together unto the supper of the great God; That ye may eat the flesh of kings, and the flesh of captains, and the flesh of mighty men, and the flesh of horses and of them that sit on them, and the flesh of all men, both free and bond, both small and great. And I saw the beast, and the kings of the earth, and their armies, gathered together to make war against him that sat on the horse, and against his army. And the beast was taken, and with him the False Prophet that wrought miracles before him, with which he deceived them and that had received the mark of the beast, and them that worshipped his image. These both were cast alive into a lake of fire burning with brimstone. And the remnant were slain with the sword of him that sat upon the horse, which sword proceeded out of his mouth; and all the fowls were filled with their flesh.

A week before Jesus was crucified, he rode a colt into Jerusalem, but now we see him riding a white horse leading an army of heavenly host to slay his enemies. He is wearing many crowns and clothed with a vesture dipped in blood. On his vesture and on his thigh there is a name written, KING OF KINGS, AND LORD OF LORDS. Out of his mouth goes a sharp sword that he will smite all nations.

There will be the greatest blood bath that the world has ever seen. An angel standing in the sun calls for all the fowls to come and gather together to eat the flesh of captains, mighty men and the flesh of horses. All the many thousands of slain men will be eaten by the fowls of the air.

The Antichrist and the False Prophet were then taken and cast alive into a burning lake of fire.

REVELATION 20:1-3 And I saw an angel come down from heaven, having the key of the bottomless pit and a great chain in his hand. And he laid hold on the dragon, that old serpent, which is the Devil, and Satan, and bound him a thousand years. And cast him into the bottomless pit, and shut him up, and sat a seal upon him, that he should deceive the nations no more, till the thousand years should be fulfilled; and after that he must be loosed a little season.

Satan is cast alive into the bottomless pit for one thousand years. John does not state in Revelation anything about all of the fallen angels and demons being cast into the bottomless pit, but they will surely be with him because of the world being without spiritual temptation during the millennial period. For one thousand years Satan will no longer roam the earth while Jesus sets up his kingdom on earth.

112 | *The Last Days*

CHAPTER NINE

THE MILLENIUM

The word millennium is not found in the bible, but it means one thousand, which is found six times in chapter 20 of the book of Revelation.

After the battle of Armageddon, and the dust is settled, Jesus will stand on the mount of Olives where he ascended from into heaven.

ACTS 1:9 And when he had spoken these things, while they beheld, he was taken up; and a cloud received him out of their sight. And while they looked steadfastly toward heaven as he went up, behold, two men stood by them in white apparel; which also said, Ye men of Galilee, why stand ye gazing up into heaven? This same Jesus, which is taken up from you into heaven, shall so come in like manner as ye have seen him go into heaven.

ZECHARIAH 14:4 And his feet shall stand in that day upon the mount of Olives, which is before Jerusalem on the east, and the mount of Olives shall cleave in the midst thereof toward the east and toward the west, and there shall be a very great valley; and half of the mountain shall remove toward the north, and half of it toward the south.

At this time He will bring all the saints with him and they will reign with him for one thousand years.

114 | *The Last Days*

REVELATION 20:4 And I saw thrones, and they sat upon them, and judgment was given unto them: and I saw the souls of them that were beheaded for the witness of Jesus, and for the word of God, and which had not worshiped the beast, neither his image, neither had received his mark upon their foreheads, or in their hands; and they lived and reigned with Christ a thousand years.

After he leaves the Mount of Olives, he will enter the temple mount where the third temple has been built before the battle of Armageddon. Some confuse this temple with the millennial temple that is described in Ezekiel where he describes the building of the fourth temple in chapters 40 through 47. The fourth temple will be huge. It, along with the walls and temple grounds, will be many square miles in diameter. The actual size is stated later in this section.

It is believed by many that when Jesus enters the temple area that he will enter the city walls from the east. There are many thoughts about this and some references of this in the bible. Some believe that one reference to this is found in Ezekiel.

EZEKIEL 44:1-3 Then he brought me back the way of the gate of the outward sanctuary which looketh toward the east; and it was shut. Then said the Lord unto me; This gate shall be shut, it shall not be opened, and no man shall enter in by it; because the Lord, the God of Israel hath entered in by it, therefore it shall be shut. It is for the prince; the prince, he shall sit in it to eat bread before the lord; he shall enter by the way of the porch of that gate, and shall go out by the way of the same.

Although many believe that this prophecy Ezekiel is speaking of is the third temple that is still standing when Jesus enters Jerusalem, I believe that this is the millennial temple that Jesus will have built during the millennium.

Another theory about Jesus entering the eastern gate is found by reading about the history of the Turks in 1517. When the Turks conquered Jerusalem under the leadership of Suleiman the Magnificent, he commanded that the city's ancient walls be rebuilt.

During this time he ordered that the Eastern Gate be sealed up with stones. No one really knows the reason for Suleiman had the gates closed, but rumors were spread in Jerusalem that the Messiah was coming and he would enter the Eastern Gate and liberate the city from the control of the foreigners. The Jewish rabbis described the Messiah as a great leader sent by God from the east. They told him that he would enter through the Eastern Gate.

Suleiman decided to close the eastern gate and have it sealed so that this would quite the Jewish hopes about the coming Lord. He also put a Muslim cemetery in front of the Eastern Gate. By doing this he believed that no Jew would defile himself by walking through a Muslim cemetery.

Today the Muslim cemetery still blocks the entrance. There are eight gates in the old walled city and only the Eastern Gate is sealed. Many sermons have been preached and songs have been written about Jesus entering through the Eastern Gate and many Jews along with Christians believe that he will enter through this gate.

While Jesus is setting up his kingdom there will be a judgment of the nations. There will be thousands of people left on earth after the battle of Armageddon who did not participate in it who are believers and non-believers. In the book of Matthew we are told of this judgment.

MATTHEW 25:32,34,41,46 When the Son of man shall come in his glory, and all the holy angels with him, then shall he sit upon the throne of his glory: And before him shall be gathered all nations: and he shall separate them one from another, as a shepherd divideth his sheep from the goats: And he shall set the sheep on his right hand, but the goats on the left. Then shall the King say unto them on his right hand, Come, ye blessed of my Father, inherit the kingdom prepared for you from the foundation of the world:

Then shall he say also unto them on the left hand, Depart from me, ye cursed, into everlasting fire, prepared for the devil and his angels.

After this judgment there will be only saved people left to inhabit the earth, along with the angels and saints with glorified bodies. They will be left to begin a brand new journey with Jesus as Ruler and King.

A scenario that hardly anyone thinks about is that the possibility of a person who is actually living now in an earthly body can live in that body forever. This could be possible and here is how it could happen. What if an unsaved person living on the earth after the rapture takes place and lives during the great tribulation and is converted at this time and is not killed by the antichrist, he would then be counted in the group of sheep that God lets continue to live on earth and enters the 1000 year period. With the long life span that would exist during this time, there would the possibility that he would live through this period and enter into the new earth that God will prepare for all believers left on earth land live forever. This is just a little food for thought.

A lot of thoughts and theories about the role of the people who have been raptured and have received their glorified bodies. Some questions are: Where will they be? What will they be doing? Will they help Jesus rule and reign over the nations?

The only indication that the bible gives is that they will reign with Christ a thousand years.

REVELATION 20:6 Blessed and holy is he who has part in the first resurrection. Over such the second death has no power, but they shall be priests of God and of Christ, and shall reign with Him a thousand years.

When a person reigns over someone, it means that they have some kind of authority over another. This could mean that the saints would lead a group of people in a nation that will be helping to rebuild cities that have been demolished during the great tribulation period. Another thought is that they could have some duty in the vast universe of God. There is one thing for certain; no one will have a dull moment while in the presence of Jesus.

We are told in the bible that there will be a multitude that no man can number that will have glorified bodies. People have often wondered what appearance the person with their glorified body would have. The Bible does not tell give us information, but we will have a body that will be perfect in every way just like Adam had when he was created. Some think that we will have the appearance of someone who would be around twenty or thirty years of age. This would be the age when normally a person is at their best physical condition. No matter how we will look, everyone will be satisfied. Just to know that this body will last forever and will never have diseases, headaches, eyes that cannot see, ears that cannot hear, crippled legs, invalids or any condition that is not perfect. The glorified body will be made to last forever.

The question is often asked about the situation of husband and wife after the rapture, what would be their relation in the world to come? How about the husband or wife who has been married to more than one spouse? Will they have multiple husbands or wives? I personally think that there will still be love for one another, but God will have a different role for each one to have in heaven. I don't believe it will be the same as it was on earth. We are told in the bible that we will be as the angels are now.

MARK 12:25 For when they shall rise from the dead, they neither marry, nor are given in marriage; but are as the angels which are in heaven.

Whatever God has planned it will completely satisfy everyone.

The makeup of the earth and heaven will have millions of saved souls, glorified bodies, angels and heavenly hosts that no one can even imagine what it will be like. Paul said that " No one can even imagine what the Lord has in store for those who love him."

Another question often asked is "Will we recognize one another in heaven?" According to the Bible we will.

1 CORINTHIANS 13:12 For now we see through a glass, darkly; but then face to face: now I know in part; but then shall I know even as also I am known.

Just as the rich man who died and was in torment recognized

Lazarus and asked him for some water. Even before we are raptured, I believe that our spirits in heaven will know one another.

The Bible does not tell us how the earth will be restored to a place where man can work and live after such a devastation of the earth during the great tribulation. When you think about all the earthquakes, rivers and seas of blood, forests that are burned, fish dead in the sea, and two thirds of the population killed by the judgments of God, you wonder how anything could even exist for long. This is just one of the things that God chose not to give us an answer right now. We know that when the Devil is released after the thousand years and the last war has been fought that God does remake the whole earth again. This will be discussed later on in this chapter. This is a subject that hardly ever is brought up in sermons or teaching today. Everyone knows that it could be restored by God with no problem by just speaking it into being.

When Jesus sets up his throne on earth, the capitol will be in Jerusalem and the government will be a theocracy, which means that he will be the supreme authority. During this period we are told that David will once again be the shepherd of the people.

EZEKIEL 34:23-24 And I will set up one shepherd over them, and he shall feed them, and he shall be their shepherd. And I the LORD will be their God, and my servant David a prince among them; I the LORD have spoken it.

EZEKIEL 37: 24-25 And David my servant shall be king over them; and they all shall have one shepherd: they shall also walk in my judgments, and observe my statutes, and do them. And they shall dwell in the land that I have given unto Jacob my servant, wherein your fathers have dwelt; and they shall dwell therein, even they, and their children, and their children's children for ever: and my servant David shall be their prince forever.

JEREMIAH 30:9 But they shall serve the LORD their God, and David their king, whom I will raise up unto them.

David will once again be King in Jerusalem and will be shepherd to his people.

We are also told that the twelve apostles will have thrones and the purpose will be to judge the twelve tribes of Israel.

MATTHEW 19:28 And Jesus said unto them, Verily I say unto you, that ye which have followed me, in the regeneration when the Son of man shall sit in the throne of his glory, ye also shall sit upon twelve thrones, judging the twelve tribes of Israel.

Jesus told the apostles that one day they would sit on thrones where they would be judges over the twelve tribes of Israel. This is the reward for giving up everything and following Jesus when he called them to go with him.

The twelve tribes of Israel will be given certain areas of land as promised by God when he told Ezekiel what land would be their inheritance.

EZEKIEL 47:13 Thus saith the Lord God; This shall be the border, whereby ye shall inherit the land according to the twelve tribes of Israel; Joseph shall have two portions.

After Jesus sets up the earthly government and David is ruling in Jerusalem along with the twelve apostles who will be governing Israel.

A lot of the great patriarchs are not mentioned during this time, such as Moses, Elijah, Elisha, Joshua, Daniel, Ezekiel and Isaiah. I am sure that they will be acting in some great authority over some area or regions of the earth.

Ever since Adam and Eve were cast out of the Garden of Eden, man has been under a curse which came about when Adam and Eve sinned. There have been struggles and hardships just as God said it would be.

GENESIS 3:17-19 And unto Adam he said, Because thou has hearkened unto the voice of thy wife, and hast eaten of the tree, of which I commanded thee, saying, Thou shalt not eat of it: cursed is the ground for thy sake; in sorrow shalt thou eat of it all the days of thy life; Thorns also and thistles shall it bring forth to thee; and thou shalt eat the herb of the field; In the sweat of thy face shalt thou eat bread, till thou return unto the ground; for out of it wast thou taken: for dust thou art, and unto dust shalt thou return.

After Jesus comes back to earth and sets up his kingdom, there will no longer be a curse on the land. There will be peace on earth at last.

There will be long life for all the people. Some people could be born at the beginning of the millennial age and still be living for a thousand years. Just as the people in the days of Noah, the life span will be very long. No one knows how many people will be alive at the start of the millennium. There could possibly be around two billion on earth. During the great tribulation we are told that two thirds of the population will be killed. Of the two billion left, possibly over half of them would be classified as "goats" and are thrown into the lake of fire. With just a million people left, with the long life that each one will have and children being born, after 1000 years there could be more inhabiting the earth than we have today.

It seems to be that God will see fit to remove all of the diseases and illnesses that we have in our day and allow people to live free of sickness and all things that farmers plant will prosper because there will be no curse on the land.

ISAIAH 65:20-22 There shall be no more thence an infant of days, nor an old man that hath not filled his days: for the child shall die an hundred years old; but the sinner being an hundred years old shall be accursed. And they shall build houses, and inhabit them; and they shall plant vineyards, and eat the fruit of them. They shall not build and another inhabit; they shall not plant, and another eat: for as the days of a tree are the days of my people, and mine elect shall long enjoy the work of their hands.

ISAIAH 2:4 And he shall judge among the nations, and shall rebuke many people and they shall beat their swords into plowshares, and their spears into pruning hooks: nation shall not lift up sword against nation, neither shall they learn war any more.

At last man can be free to go about farming and other jobs without the threat of war. After the earth has been cleaned up and everyone is living a Christian life, it will be so much of a blessing to see crops in the field giving tremendous yield without the curse being upon it. Everything that man will do will be blessed by Jesus who will be King on earth.

We are told that even the animals of the world will become vegetarians and will not eat meat anymore or will they harm anyone for they will be as gentle as lambs.

ISAIAH 11:6-9 The wolf also shall dwell with the lamb, and the leopard shall lie down with the kid; and the calf and the young lion and the fatling together, and a little child shall lead them. And the cow and the bear shall feed; their young ones shall lie down together: and the lion shall eat straw like the ox. And the sucking child shall play on the hole of the asp, and the weaned child shall put his hand on the cockatrice' den. They shall not hurt nor destroy in all my holy mountain: for the earth shall be full of the knowledge of the LORD as the waters cover the sea.

There is a song that is sung today called "Peace in the Valley." This will literally come true during the millennium. There will be no fear of man nor beast in the whole world once Jesus is the reigning King.

ZECHARIAH 8:3-5 Thus saith the LORD; I am returned unto Zion, and will dwell in the midst of Jerusalem: and Jerusalem shall be called a city of truth; and the mountain of the LORD of hosts the holy mountain. Thus saith the LORD of hosts; There shall yet old men and old women dwell in the streets of Jerusalem, and every man with his staff in his hand for very age. And the streets of the city shall be full of boys and girls playing in the streets thereof.

In the book of Ezekiel we are told that there will be a millennial temple built for people to come and worship Jesus. This will be a temple that will surpass anything that has ever been built in size and beauty. King Solomon built the first temple and it was a thing of beauty with all its gold plated walls and items used by the king. In today's cost it would run into the billions.

At some time the third temple that is built by the Jews before the great tribulation will be torn down during the reign of Jesus and a fourth temple will be built just as God laid out the plans in the book of Ezekiel beginning with Chapter 40 through 48.

The millennial temple and temple grounds will literally dwarf the other temples when compared in size. The Bible uses cubits when stating the size of objects and land. The cubit is about 18 inches in length. The temple area when converted to miles is about 8 1/3 miles square.

EZEKIEL 48:20 All the oblation shall be five and twenty thousand by five and twenty thousand: ye shall offer the holy oblation foursquare, with the possession of the city.

The actual size of the city walls will be 1 ½ miles square. There will be three gates on each side with the names of three tribes of Israel on each side. The land for the temple will be 875 feet square. The complete layout of the temple and furnishings are found in Ezekiel, chapters 40 through 48.

The temple rituals and sacrificial offerings will again take place just as they were when the first temple was built. The sacrifices that are offered will be as a memorial to the real sacrifice that was given by Jesus on the cross. This will not be an offering for salvation, because Jesus paid the price on the cross and brought about grace and eternal salvation for all who believe on his name.

All children who are born to believers will still be given the opportunity to receive Christ as their savior because of the free will that is given them. It is true that Satan is bound during this 1000 year period, but the old nature is still a part of the earthly beings.

As the millennial age comes to a close there will be a multitude of people who have not became believers. Just as Adam and Eve had a utopia in the Garden of Eden and sinned, so will a vast number of people in the millennial age do the same thing. People who had everything one could want but still gave in to the old nature that existed in every earthly human from the time of Adam and Eve.

This is the time that Satan is released from the bottomless pit.

No one really knows why Satan is released to organize another army against God's people, but God had a plan and sometimes we don't quite understand it, but it is always perfect, for God is perfect.

REVELATION:7-8 And when the thousand years are expired, Satan shall be loosed out of his prison. And shall go out to deceive the nations which are in the four quarters of the earth, Gog, and Magog, to gather them together to battle: the number of whom is as the sand of the sea.

Satan will once again be the same evil being that he was when he was cast into the bottomless pit and will deceive nations from all over the earth to follow him. Gog and Magog who came against Israel sometime before the great tribulation will team up with him and will be ready to make war on the beloved city, which is Jerusalem. This is very much like the nations which came upon Jerusalem during the battle of Armageddon.

REVELATION 20:9 And they went up on the breadth of the earth, and compassed the camp of the saints about, and the beloved city: and fire came down from God out of heaven, and devoured them.

This battle is a very short one because God sends fire down from heaven and devours them. The description of this battle is very short. It takes only three verses to tell the whole story how God destroys the enemy.

Satan's evil reign finally comes to an end. The angelic being who was once the most beautiful and brilliant arch angel in God's domain is now being cast into the lake of fire that God had prepared for him and his angels.

REVELATION 20:10 And the Devil that deceived them was cast into the lake of fire and brimstone, where the Beast and the False Prophet are, and shall be tormented day and night forever and ever.

This verse answers the question that a lot of people have asked concerning the dead in the lake of fire. It tells us that the Beast and

False Prophet are still there after over one thousand years. Did they burn up? No! How can anything just burn forever? My answer would be that we don't know and perhaps one day God will reveal it to us.

After this the apostle John describes the next scene that takes place.

THE GREAT WHITE THRONE JUDGMENT

REVELATION 20:11-15 And I saw a great white throne, and him that sat on it, from whose face the earth and the heaven fled away; and there was found no place for them. And I saw the dead, small and great, stand before God; and the books were opened: and another book was opened, which is the book of life: and the dead were judged out of those things which were written in the books, according to their works. And the sea gave up the dead, which were in it; and death and hell delivered up the dead which were in them: and they were judged every man according to their works. And death and hell were cast into the lake of fire. This is the second death. And whosoever was not found written in the book of life was cast into the lake of fire.

At this time all of the lost from the time of Adam until this judgment takes place will now stand before God. Up until this time, the souls of the unbelievers were kept in the inner parts of the earth in a place of torment called "Hades". Some will have been there for over seven thousand years. Millions upon millions will be resurrected from this place and stand before God for final sentencing. All who stand before God at the great white throne will be cast into the lake of fire because their names are not found in the book of life. This will be like a convicted murderer that has been jail for a long period and finally stands before the judge for the final sentence.

This will be the most horrible time that mankind has ever witnessed. This is a time when every knee shall bow before God as stated in the scripture. Romans 14:11 - For it is written, As I live, saith the Lord, every knee shall bow to me, and every tongue shall confess to God.

As each name is called out to see if their name is written in the book of life and when it is not found, it will be the saddest day they have ever witnessed. They will then be cast into the lake of fire to stay forever.

We do not know where the lake of fire is located. Some even say that we as saints will get to witness this event. No one knows but God. In the vast universe of God I'm sure it will be in the right place

I am sure that everyone will have some kind of excuse for their prior actions, but it will be too late to bring it up. This is called the second death.

This will bring to a close to the life on earth as we know it today. John explains the future life in the next chapter.

CHAPTER TEN

THE NEW HEAVEN AND EARTH

After the great white judgment is over and Satan and all his angels and demons along with all the ones whose name was not found in the book of life are cast into the lake of fire, John gives us another look into the future at things that are to take place.

REVELATION 21:1 And I saw a new heaven and a new earth: for the first heaven and the first earth were passed away; and there was no more sea.

The earth as we know it now will still be filled with billions of people who received Christ as Savior before the millennial age started and the ones who were saved during the one thousand years. The millennial temple will still be in existence, Jesus will still be reigning as King and David and all the apostles and patriarchs will still be leading the people. The question is asked so many times, how will a new earth and new heaven be brought into existence? In 2 Peter 3:10-13 it gives a statement regarding this.

2 PETER 3:10-13 But the day of the Lord will come as a thief in the night; in the which the heavens shall pass away with a great noise, and the elements shall melt with fervent heat, the earth also and the works that are therein shall be burned up. Seeing then that all these things shall be dissolved, what manner of persons out ye to be in all holy conversation and godlines. Looking for and hasting unto the coming of the day of God, wherein the heavens being on

fire shall be dissolved, and the elements shall melt with fervent heat? Neverless we, according to his promise, look for new heavens and a new earth, wherein dwelleth righteousness.

This passage of scripture is one that I think that only God could give us the steps that He will take when all this takes place.

Some will say that God will just change the present earth and refine it where it will a paradise. Others will say that the earth will never be destroyed, but in the book of Matthew we read in chapter 24:35 that "heaven and earth will pass away, but my words shall not pass away". There we have the very words of Jesus telling us that they will pass away.

The questions so many have and still no legitimate answer is " Where will all the earthly people be while all this is taking place?" "Will they be in the Holy City?" How long will this process of creating a new heaven and earth take place?" Some preachers and theologians have come up with some kind of answers, but cannot say that this is the exact way it will all happen.

Some have said that all the earthly beings along with the saints with glorified bodies will simply be transported the Holy City and be in it when God brings it down to the new earth. This would be about the only logical way that our small minds could comprehend.

The bottom line is that God has a plan and however He sees fit to bring about all the new creation of a new heaven and earth will be perfect. The main thing for us to dwell on is to make sure that our names are written in the Lambs book of Life where we will be with Jesus when all of this takes place.

So God has created a new heaven and a new earth and the old heaven and earth is passed away. This will be by far the one of the most magnificent creations that God has done thus far.

Revelation 21:1 tells us that there will be no more sea. The question is asked "why would there be no more sea?" The answer could be that the sea would no longer needed for earthly beings to use as a way of travel and food to eat from the sea. Again, as stated before, God has it worked out and it is perfect.

What will the size of the new earth be? No one knows, but it will all be land and it will still be cultivated and farmed with no kind of curse upon it. It will still have the billions of earthly people upon it and will last forever.

Jesus told his disciples that he was going away and preparing a place for them and would come again. He said that in his Father's house are many mansions. This is what he is talking about in Revelation 21:2-6 And I John saw the Holy City, New Jerusalem, coming down from God out of heaven, prepared as a bride adorned for her husband. And I heard a great voice out of heaven saying, Behold, the tabernacle of God is with men, and he will dwell with them, and they shall be his people, and God himself shall be with them and be their God. And God shall wipe away all tears from their eyes; and there shall be no more death, neither sorrow, nor crying, neither shall there be any more pain: for the former things are passed away. He that sat upon the throne said, Behold, I make all things new and he said unto me, write; these words are true and faithful. And he said unto me, It is done. I am Alpha and Omega, the beginning and the end; I will give unto him that is athirst of the fountain of the water of life freely.

John sees the holy city coming down out of heaven and coming towards earth. God tells him that He will have his tabernacle among men and dwell with them forever. Can you imagine what John was thinking when he saw this city? He probably remembered Jesus telling the apostles about him going away and preparing a place for them. He never once imagined anything like this site.

God tells him that from now on everything is going to be all right. He will wipe away all tears from every eye. Up until now man had shed tears over lost love ones and physical harm to their bodies. Even during the millennium there was death and some of their loved ones would not turn to Christ. Some will say "How can I still be happy in heaven when someone I loved is lost and will never see them again?" No one knows the answer. We can only trust God and take his word that he will do what he has promised.

It is really hard sometimes for a person to really comprehend about the fact that they will be living with God for eternity. This means not just a million years, but a never ending life. A life where there will be no more dying, no more poverty, no more worrying about the welfare of a family, no more sickness, no doctors to see about a disease and no money worries because everything is taken care of by God himself, for he will be on his throne with Jesus at his right hand.

We will probably travel about the vast universe that we can only see just a tiny part of that never ends. There could be planets out there that are inhabited by someone and it could be our job to look over them. The possibilities of things to come have never entered into our small minds. All that we need to know is that it will be perfect from a perfect God.

In today's life, everyone is always concerned about the safety and protection of family from robbers, murderers, rapists, liars and other people who would hurt and cause worry in one's life. The next verse assures us that all of this has been taken care of.

REVELATION 21:8 But the fearful, and unbelieving, and the abominable, and murderers, and whoremongers, and sorcerers, and idolaters, and all liars, shall have their part in the lake which burneth with fire and brimstone: which is the second death.

All of the above mentioned has all ready been taken care of at the great white throne judgment, which was the second death. This judgment cleansed the earth and heaven of anything that would offend or hurt anyone anymore.

Then an angel told John to come hither and I will show you the bride, the Lamb's wife.

REVELATION 21:9-10 And there came unto me one of the seven angels which had the seven vials full of the seven last plagues, and talked with me, saying, Come hither, I will shew thee the bride, the Lamb's wife. And he carried me away in the spirit to a great and high mountain, and shewed me that great city, the holy Jerusalem, descending out of heaven from God. Having the glory of God and her light was like unto a stone most precious, even like a jasper stone, clear as crystal.

At this time John saw the most amazing sight that he had ever seen. The huge city coming down from heaven. This was the Lamb's wife. At church weddings, the bride always wants to look the very best for her husband to be and does everything to make the wedding just right. The same thing is happening here. The holy city coming down has been prepared for Jesus and is magnificent. The contents of this city is inhabited by the glorified saints and who are already living in this great city. They already have their rooms and have been welcomed in by the Lord himself.

Now comes the time to make everything official. The marriage has taken place. The marriage supper of the Lamb is about to take place. Everyone who has their name written in the Lambs book of Life has been called to the marriage feast. Everything is completed and everyone is ready to start living forever with Jesus as King of Kings and Lord of Lords.

At this point in John's vision, he is carried upon a high mountain and sees the most magnificent of any city that he has ever seen. The city is so huge that he can only see a portion of it at a time. He begins to see the walls and foundations of this tremendous city and the angel tells him the size of the walls and the city and what it is made up of.

REVELATION 11:18 Having the glory of God and her light was like unto a stone most precious, even like a jasper stone, clear as crystal; And had a wall great and high, and had twelve gates, and at the gates twelve angels, and names written theron, which are the names of the twelve tribes of the children of Israel: On the east three gates; on the north three gates: on the south three gates, and on the west three gates. And the wall of the city had twelve foundations, and in them the names of the twelve apostles of the Lamb. And he that talked with me had a golden reed to measure the city, and the gates thereof, and the wall thereof. And the city lieth foursquare, and the length is as large as the breadth: and he measured the city and the reed, twelve thousand furlongs. The length and the breadth and the height of it are equal. And he measured the wall thereof, an hundred and forty and four cubits, according the measure of a man that is of the angel. And the building of the wall of it was of jasper: and the city was pure gold, like unto clear glass.

The walls of the city are jasper, which is a gem that is red in color and very beautiful.

REVELATION 21:19-20 And the foundations of the wall of the city were garnished with all manner of precious stones. The first foundation was jasper, the second, sapphire, the third, a chalcedony; the fourth, an emerald; The fifth, sardonic; the sixth, sardius; the seventh, chrysolite, the eighth, beryl; the ninth, a topaz; the tenth, a chrysoprasus; the eleventh, a jacinth; the twelfth, amethyst. And the twelve gates were twelve pearls: every several gate was of one pearl: and the street of the city was pure gold, as it were transparent glass.

Most of the time in modern day, foundations of walls and buildings, are made up of cement, blocks, bricks and sometimes marble. The walls of the Holy City would have twelve foundations made up of solid gems and precious stones to hold up a wall of pure gold.

One of the first things that John noticed was the high walls, which were about two hundred and sixteen feet high. When referring to measurements in the Bible it always it uses the word cubit. The cubit measurement is considered to be the distance from a man's elbow to the tip of his fingers, which is about eighteen inches in our measurement of today.

The walls, when converted to our present day scale, were fifteen hundred miles per wall in length. This would make it fifteen hundred miles square.

There were twelve gates that were made of twelve pearls. This would be unbelievable to see pearls that were made into a gate that was over two hundred feet high. They will be located about every five hundred miles. Each one of them would have the names of the twelve tribes of Israel over them. Each gate would have angels standing by it.

The city was pure gold, although it was like clear glass. This is something out of the ordinary and we can't even imagine how this would look. Even the streets are pure gold.

The height of the Holy City was also fifteen hundred miles. The height of the city has brought about many questions over the ages. It is really hard to visualize any kind of structure being that tall. Some have said that it is made like a cube, with the center being the highest point. Others have said it would be one mountain range after another until it rose to a height of fifteen hundred miles.

A popular belief nowadays is that the city would just hover over the earth at a distance of fifteen hundred miles. With this city being that far away it would appear to someone on earth about the size of the moon, because the moon is just a little larger than the Holy City. If this was the location, traveling would be through space from earth to the city and back again.

If a city of this size was placed in a country the size of The United States, it would reach from Maine to Florida, to Colorado and on to Canada.

When you think about a foundation, you think of some substance that will be placed on the ground for a building or a house. The Holy City will be sitting on a foundation of precious stones. It would seem that if it was suspended in the air over the earth there would be no need for a foundation. This is the reason I believe that it will be sitting on the new earth for people to come into and go out.

When the earth is renewed or created anew, we cannot say just how large it will be. We do know that if God places the Holy City on earth it will have plenty of room to set on and will be perfect.

How many people could a city of this size hold? Some have come up with an estimate of one hundred billion. This would be a figure that we could not even visualize. There will be other structures other than mansions for the people to enjoy. We read about this a little later

REVELATION 21:22 And I saw no temple therein: for the Lord God Almighty and the Lamb are the temple of it.

The new city will not have a temple, but I believe that there will be a throne in the midst for God to sit on and probably other thrones for all the patriarchs to sit on as they did during the millennium.

REVELATION 21:23-24 And the city had no need of the sun, neither of the moon, to shine in it: for the glory of God did lighten it, and the Lamb is the light thereof. And the nations of them which are saved shall walk in the light of it; and the kings of the earth do bring their glory and honor into it.

REVELATION 21:25 And the gates of it shall not be shut at all by day; for there shall be no night there.

I have often heard people say that if they did not have to sleep at night they could get a lot done. This will be a period of time when this will happen. One might ask these questions? Will there be any need for calendars, alarm clocks or watches? Time as we know it today will not exist in the afterlife in heaven.

The world will walk in the light of the Holy City and the saved people who once inhabited the old earth will once again go back to their normal everyday routine of working and having families just as they did in the millennium. The one exception is that there is no evil spirit or temptation to do wrong for Satan and all of his angels and demons are in the lake of fire and they will have no effect on anyone anymore.

A question comes in about day and night. We are told in Rev. 21: 3 that the city had no need of light because the light came from the presence of God and the Lamb. Notice the word "need" of the sun or moon anymore. It does not say that there will not be any sun or moon, it is just that there is no need of them in the city.

Could it be that outside of the city there would be a need for the earthly beings who are working and farming to have the light and the seasons for their work to be successful? We are told in Genesis 8:22 that "While the earth remaineth seedtime and harvest, and cold and heat, and summer and winter, and day and night shall not cease." Some would say that these verses contradict one another. This would not be the case. In verse 22 above it states that as long as the earth remains. The earth that will be in existence then will be a new one, so the old earth remains no longer.

The bottom line is that it does not really matter. If there is no sun or moon for the earthly beings, the light from the Holy City will do just fine for God will be in control just as He is now.

Nothing that is unholy or unpure will never enter the holy city, because all evil is in the lake of fire and will never be able to tempt anyone to sin forever.

REVELATION 21:27 And there shall in no wise enter into it anything that defileth, neither whatsoever worketh abomination, or maketh a lie: but they which are written in the Lamb's book of life.

The apostle John now takes a journey inside the holy city and relates to us what he sees in this vast city.

REVELATION 22:1-2 And he showed me a pure river of water of life, clear as crystal, proceeding out of the throne of God and of the Lamb. In the midst of the street of it, and on either side of the river, was there the tree of life, which bare twelve manner of fruits, and yielded her fruit every month: and the leaves of the tree were for the healing of the nations.

On the earth today there are many clear springs and rivers that are real clear and are beautiful to look at, but is nothing to compare to the crystal river in the holy city. The river probably runs the length of the city and proceeds out of the throne of God and Jesus. We can only imagine the beauty of this river. There's no mud on the bottom, no logs or limbs to blemish the sight of this crystal masterpiece. The question will be asked I'm sure "Will there be any fish in the crystal river?" No one knows but God. If they are, it might look like a huge aquarium or something of that nature.

In the winter time, there is an occasional ice storm where all of the tree tops are frozen with ice. All the trees look like crystal and this is such a beautiful sight. I believe that inside the Holy City will be scenes like these only more beautiful.

Very little is said about the other things of the city, but there are some things that will not be there such as:

No power lines along the streets, because electricity will not be needed there.

No automobiles, buses, railroads or subways, because travel will be controlled by the power Jesus gives us.

No clothing stores, because we will have garments that will last forever.

No hospitals, because there will never be any sickness or accidents forever.

No restaurants or grocery stores, because the heavenly food that will be available in the city.

No insurance companies and funeral homes, because no one will ever die.

No building supply stores, because the Holy City is finished and will never need any repair.

No beauty salons and barber shops, because everyone will have perfect bodies.

No banks or Wall Street trading, because no one will ever have any need for money, everything is furnished.

No law offices or politicians, because Jesus is ruler over all.

No TV, telephone, or computer stores, because everyone will have their own communication system stored in their glorified body and will have no need for them anymore.

No heating or air condition stores, because the temperature will be perfect all the time.

No military bases, because God will have everything under control and will never have any wars any more.

No airports, because air travel will be unlike anything we can even imagine, through God's power plan.

It will be strange not having a Wal-Mart to go to, but we can rest assured the Holy City will have something even better.

Questions are asked all the time by Christians, "Will we be able to go fishing in heaven?" God may provide us with this privilege or he may have something different for us to do that we would enjoy more than fishing and trying to catch the big one. We will not be disappointed whatever happens for God has only the best in store for those he loves.

In the midst of the streets and on each side of the river is the tree of life. In the scripture the tree is written singular, but these trees will be on each side of the river and will reach for hundreds of miles along the river. In the Garden of Eden, the tree of life existed along with the tree of knowledge of good and evil. After Adam and Eve ate from the tree of knowledge of good and evil, God decided to cast them out of the Garden of Eden because if they ate from the tree of life they would live forever.

This tree bares twelve kinds of fruit and yields fruit every month. This could be a fruit that is eaten by all the heavenly saints or even by the earthly beings that come in and out of the holy city.

The leaves are for the healing of the nations. This is not to insinuate that anyone needs a medicine to keep them from being sick, but it could be a kind of refreshing balm that would give energy when needed.

Some believe that the earthly beings will come in each month and pick these leaves for continued life. This is a gray area and no one can really say how they will be used.

The main question that most people ask about heaven is "What will we do?" They are a lot of theories and thoughts about what everyone will be doing in the hereafter. We will surely spend a lot of time just worshipping and praising God. Some of the angels that John saw were continually praising God without ceasing. We will have plenty of time to praise and worship God for we will not need anytime to sleep and time will not be measured any more.

We could spend a lot of time just relaxing by the crystal river, not that we would be tired, but just admiring the handiwork of God.

We could be taking a journey through the universe and visiting the billions of galaxies that exist. No one can really comprehend a universe that does not have an end to it.

This is just another of the many things that God has created to our amazement.

The main thing that everyone will be so thrilled and happy is just being able to see and talk with Jesus where we can spend a lot of time just thanking him for saving us and giving us a place like this to spend through all eternity.

No one can hardly visualize how this new earth and the Holy City will look like, but we will be happy to be there and know we will live there forever.

CONCLUSION

I hope this book has been a blessing to you in some way. If you are a Christian, the last chapter tells of the blessings we will have while we spend eternity with our Lord and Savior Jesus Christ. This will be a glorious time just to have the assurance of being with Jesus and never again have any sorrows and sickness.

If you are not a Christian I hope that you will read the passages of scripture below that tells you how to obtain eternal life by receiving Jesus as your Lord and Savior.

ROMANS 3:23 All have sinned, and come short of the glory of God.

ROMANS 6:23 The wages of sin is death; but the gift of God is eternal life through Jesus Christ our Lord.

REVELATION 20:15 And whosoever was not found written in the book of life was cast into the lake of fire.

JOHN 3:16 For God so loved the world, that he gave his only begotten Son, that whosoever believeth in him should not perish, but have everlasting life.

Romans 10:9-10 That if thou shalt confess with thy mouth the Lord Jesus, and shalt believe in thine heart that God has raised him from the dead, thou shalt be saved. For with the heart man believeth unto righteousness and with the mouth confession is made unto salvation.

Remember that Jesus is coming soon.